Astrology Sex Diet

by Ariella Moonstone

with Vivian Woodley, MA, MFT
and Ray Dabar, CN

Cover layout by Lisa Ponder
Edited by Catherine Gigante-Brown
Produced by Vinnie Corbo

Volossal
Publishing

Published by Volossal Publishing
www.volossal.com

Copyright © 2012
ISBN 978-0-9968826-6-8

Table of Contents

Introduction

Imagine, feeling completely satisfied, satiated and happy with yourself and your life. How? By being true to who you are and honoring the traits of your Sun Sign. As an astrologer, I'm a firm believer that most of our troubles stem from fighting (or even ignoring) the natural propensities dictated by our stars. Ask a Leo to be vegetarian and trouble ensues—and not just of the gastronomic nature. Expect a Pisces not to flirt, and they're totally miserable trying to live up to that impossibility.

I am 100% convinced that following your path in the Zodiac is the road to a joyful, complete, totally-fulfilled existence. The *Astrology Sex Diet* will show you how, why—and help guide you along that path.

> - Ariella Moonstone
> *Sedona, 2012*

Astrology, Sex and Diet

The seed for this book was sewn many years ago when an acquaintance (who happens to be a librarian) mentioned to me that the three most common types of books stolen from libraries are about:

astrology
diet,
and sex

For some reason, I never forgot this perplexing tidbit. What is it about this trio that is so shameful, so secretive, and yet so captivating that people must resort to thievery to get them? Were the three topics somehow related? And if so, how? I was compelled to uncover the answer.

As an astrologer for two decades and counting, I knew full well how the stars, planets and our Sun Signs played a strong role in our destinies. Similarly, what we put into our bodies— figuratively and literally—fuels us and helps propel each of us along our respective lifepaths. And sex, well, let's face it...sex rules everything! It obsesses us, upsets us, thrills us, guides us, and can even destroy us if we don't have a healthy attitude about our erotic selves.

Why do we gravitate toward certain foods—be it spicy or sweet, bland or savory? Why do we find ourselves with a particular man or woman time and time again—the bad seed, the good egg, fiery siren or safe nerd? Why do we prefer certain sex positions or have favorite acts that others might find repugnant, or even kinky? And do our astrological signs have anything to do with this?

I decided to pose these questions to my dear friends, licensed psychologist Vivian Woodley, and nutritionist Ray Dabar, to invite their opinions concerning whether or not these three visceral areas—astrology, sex and diet—are related. Several passionate discussions ensued. Lots of note-taking, soul-searching and passionate writing followed. The result of which, you are holding in your hot, little hand-held: The *Astrology Sex Diet*.

So, are you ready to change your life? Well, we're ready to guide you.

About Us

Ariella Moonstone, Astrologist, Libra

Born in the heart of Sedona, Arizona's breathtaking Red Rock Country, Ariella Moonstone was destined to be an astrologer from the very start. Perhaps it was the lush carpet of stars overhead that lulled her to sleep each night, but she had an early fascination with the heavens above. Beginning with her favorite tome, *Linda Goodman's Sun Signs*, Ariella began devouring all of the astrology books she could find and soon was charting the stars of friends, family and even the family dog, with uncanny accuracy. She has been a much-sought after professional in the field for several decades with many recognizable names among her private clientele. Ariella loves to travel, especially to spiritually-charged, magnetic centers of the globe—Stonehenge, India and her funky little hometown are among her favorites.

Vivian Woodley, MA MFT, Taurus

As a licensed therapist for more than 20 years, Vivian Woodley has seen clients who need help coping with a variety of important issues, from dealing with grief to lack of self-esteem and depression. With her kindness, compassion and patient ear, Vivian is also an expert in the area of marriage counseling. Over the years, she's come to specialize in issues sexual, more specifically in the area of fetish and what some perceive to be sexual deviancy. Non-judgmental, supportive and always positive, our resident blonde bombshell combines professional expertise with a more-than-palatable bedside manner, contributing to the sexual side of the *Astrology Sex Diet* equation. Vivian and her husband of twenty years live in Southern California.

Ray Dabar, CN, Sagittarius

Supplying the testosterone to the creative triad, Certified Nutritionist Ray Dabar has been a respected wellness warrior and educator since 1999. He has provided nutrition programs for diverse groups of people with an emphasis on long-term follow-up and support programming. Ray has developed thousands of food plans for his clients—from Hollywood A-listers and professional athletes to businessmen and everyone else in between—in the areas of sports nutrition, weight management, eating disorder recovery disease prevention and wellness. Ray is a breath of fresh air in a field that can be confusing and contradictory. His nutrition philosophy looks at the total person, spiritually as well as physically. Sporting a "to-die-for" six-pack, Ray is an avid swimmer, cyclist, skier and runner, and lives in Woodstock, New York.

How To Use This Book

We've taken great care to create the *Astrology Sex Diet* in such a way that it will make sense to those who aren't experts in the fields of astrology, sexology and nutrition. Even if this is the first book you've ever picked up in any of the above subject areas, we've crafted it so that it will speak plainly to you and be of great use. No need to understand complex star charts, know the food pyramid inside out or be well versed in the signs of sexual addiction. We've written it in layman's terms so that everyone can understand it and benefit from it. And we also think that it doesn't hurt to be a little playful (and even a bit naughty!) in the process. After all, we want you to laugh as well as learn.

The Set-Up

The *Astrology Sex Diet* is arranged by astrological sign, starting with Aries, which spans from March 21 through April 20. Historically, Aries has been considered the first sign of the Zodiac because it signifies the beginning of spring (in the western world, at least), and is the symbol of birth and beginnings. Also, in ancient Roman times, March was the first month of the year. Until 46BC, when Julius Caesar changed Month Numero Uno to January. (But hey, if you christen yourself with the lofty title "Prefect of the Morals," you have license to do just about anything, right?) But by then, the Zodiac calendar was well established and Aries was still considered Sun Sign # 1.

11

Within each Zodiac sign, we start by giving a low-down of its characteristics, then zoom in on bedroom proclivities, and lastly information on diet and food.

But no matter what your Sun Sign happens to be, we encourage you to read the entire ebook so you can appreciate and better understand your friends, lovers and even your enemies from across the Zodiac.

A Note on Astrological Dates

You may have already noticed that the start and end dates of astrological signs vary greatly according to the astrologer. Some might list Taurus as spanning from April 20 through May 20, while others mark it as running from April 21 through May 21. In my experience, I've found these hard and fast dates to be of little importance. But for the sake of clarity, we've used the dates established by my Sun Signs goddess Linda Goodman.

However, if you were born on the first or last day of an astrological sign, you were born on what we call "the cusp." Traditionally, children of the cusp often have attributes of both signs. If you're a cusper, you will probably benefit from reading about your Sun Sign and the Sun Sign that ends or begins right before or after your date of birth. So, if you're born on April 20 like my significant other, your actual Sun Sign is Aries, (according to Ms. Goodman, et al), but you might have some Taurus traits as well. Other astrologers hold fast to Aries as ending on April 19, and Taurus beginning on April 20, but in the case of my guy, he is 100% stubborn ram thrill-seeker all the way! So cuspers are advised to read the attributes of both Sun Signs in question and decide which child of the Zodiac they most resemble.

A Note on Diet

It's no secret that different Sun Signs prefer different types of nourishment. In fact, when they go against that grain, digestive disturbances and weight gain almost always occur. We're not saying that dessert-loving Libras (like Ariella!) can survive and thrive on nothing but chocolate cake but their systems tend to tolerate sweets better than, say, a salad-loving Virgo. Likewise, the carnivore-heavy diet of a Taurean might turn the stomach of seafoodies like Pisces and Aquarius. Ray has guided us with diet preferences that both work for and are natural for each Sun Sign. So the message here is to be true to your food for a happier, healthy you.

However, we also stress that it's important to eat a balanced diet from all of the food groups to ensure that you are getting all the nutrients you need to maintain a fit lifestyle. This is why you will notice a number of food choices which will appeal to, and are beneficial to, particular Sun Signs. E.g. high-protein foods for Sagittarians and a selection of fruits and veggies even a Leo will love.

Let's Talk About Sex

Some of you might remember those cheesy "Sex Positions of the Zodiac" posters from the 1970s. Well…we're not going there. Any discussion of sex will be kept adult and intelligent, yet frank and up front. Dr. Vivian insists!

Okay, now we're good to go!

Disclaimer

This book is intended for entertainment purposes only. Please consult a physician before changing your diet or your lifestyle.

Crash Course In Astrology 101

Elements

The Sun Signs are grouped into four essential elements which, when combined, create a balanced world and allow life to flourish. Each of the 12 astrological signs is associated with a specific element which further helps us to understand our place in the planet.

The four astrological elements are:

- **Fire** – Fire people tend to be impulsive, and just like the way fire spreads, they often leap before they look. The three Fire Signs are: *Aries, Leo* and *Sagittarius.*

- **Water** – Water folk come in two varieties: they can be contained like a pond or they can rage like a flood. The three Water Signs are: *Cancer, Scorpio* and *Pisces.*

- **Earth** – Earth Signs are very grounded and "real" since earth is the foundation upon which everything is built. The three Earth Signs are: *Taurus, Virgo* and *Capricorn.*

- **Air** – Individuals born under Air Signs tend to be as elusive and unpredictable as the wind, yet air is also an extremely necessary element as it fuels fire, feeds the earth and ventilates water. The three Air Signs are: *Gemini, Libra* and *Aquarius.*

Heavenly Bodies

The 12 signs of the Zodiac are each given a heavenly body that rules their destiny. People born under that sign often have attributes of that planet, star or moon. Case in point, the mood of a changeable Moon Child or Cancer can fluctuate more than the tide or a sun-ruled Leo usually has the temperament as fiery as our closest star.

We made a conscious decision not to get into Qualities (Cardinal, Fixed, Mutable) or Polarities (negative and positive) because they're simply too confusing for the average bear.

Stones

There are also a dozen stones affiliated with each Sun Sign. Many, like opal for Libra, are the same as birthstones for corresponding months (October, in this case, as Libra occurs mostly during this month), while others are not. Early civilizations, like those in India and Babylon, gave gemstones magical properties. Over time, astrologers assigned gems of particular colors to the 12 signs of the Zodiac to help people influence the planets in their favor.

Enter first century Jewish historian Josephus, who proclaimed a connection between the 12 stones in Aaron's (Moses' big brother) breastplate, the 12 months of the year and the 12 signs of the Zodiac. There have been many translations and interpretations of the passage in Exodus which refers to Aaron's magnificent breastplate, and these interpretations vary a great deal. Josephus himself gives two different lists for the 12 stones.

16

Confusing? Yes! Which accounts for different astrologers naming different "official" stones of the Zodiac. The stones noted here are the ones Ariella's used for eons, and we're sticking to them!

Symbols, Lifequests, Vibes, Dirty Little Secrets, Bodyparts, Fuelfoods, Sign Songs and Movies

To keep things interesting, in addition to all of the above—Elements, Heavenly Bodies and Stones—we've also included Symbols, Lifequests, Vibes, Dirty Little Secrets, Bodyparts (exactly what it sounds like—bodyparts that rule each Sun Sign) and what we call Fuelfoods for all of the Sun Signs. They're all pretty much self explanatory.

To multiply the funfactor, we've noted Sign Songs and signature Movies for each member of the Zodiac. (More about them in the following section.) Think of these headers as your quick Sun Sign reference guide.

Then we get into the nitty-gritty, describing general attributes (All About...), erotic characteristics (...Between the Sheets) and food preferences (Diet).

More About Sign Songs & Movies

For your entertainment pleasure, we thought "Sign Songs" might be an amusing addition for each astrological sign. These are musical selections which seem to perfectly illustrate the traits of each Zodiac sign. Ditto for movies which we feel capture the spirit of the sign.

Aries
March 21 - April 20

Element: Fire

Heavenly Body: Mars

Symbol: The Ram

Stone: Ruby

Lifequest: A thrill a minute

Vibe: Passionate

Dirty Little Secret: I like to do the driving—and fast!

Bodypart: The head

Fuelfoods: Hot and spicy rules, especially ethnic foods like Indian and Mexican cuisines, the hotter the better

Sign Song: "Like a Rock"

Movie: *Firestarter*—This flick about a pint-sized gal who can start fires with her ire strikes a chord with this smoldering Sun Sign.

All About Aries

These fiery individuals are regarded as the most adventurous of the Zodiac. Extremely active and physical, Aries are happiest when they're scaring the tuna salad out of themselves. They're always up for a challenge, the more terrifying and more nail-biting, the better. Rock-climbing, downhill skiing (fast!), motorcycle and car-racing (faster!) are all attractive sports to the Aries. Did we mention that they're speed-junkies? Hands down, Ariens will have the most florid collection of speeding tickets — or the best stories about how they charmed their way out of them.

Although Aries folks tend not to favor organized sports like softball or football, they are thrill-seekers supreme. Daredevils, yes, but they generally don't charge in thoughtlessly without carefully considering the situation and all of the variables.

Ditto for getting off of their guff and making a move. Those born under this Sun Sign are commonly criticized for being procrastinators supreme but that's not exactly the case. An Aries must look at all sides of the equation (and argument) before taking a stand, but when they do something, it's firmly and resolutely. And good luck convincing them to change their ram-like stance!

But despite their wild physical abandon, Aries is also a distinctively naïve sign. They're not childlike but more closely, children at heart.

On the one hand, they are independent, gregarious and confident, but on the other hand, they are *tres* trusting. Perhaps too trusting. Because you can entrust an Aries with your life and all your deepest darkest secrets, that's exactly what they expect from everyone else. It's not always what they get, however. So unsuspecting are the Aries breed that they can unwittingly walk into the snake pit—and then are super surprised when they get bitten.

But fear not, Aries also has the uncanny ability to rebound emotionally and physically, whatever the challenge. Their supreme trust should be considered a strength rather than a weakness because they manage to come out triumphant over whatever they confront.

Aries never give up, no matter what. They're the ones you want by your side in an emergency or during a disaster because not only do they keep a clear head but they maintain a positive attitude—and darned if they don't see you through to the light at the end of the tunnel. Yes, the amazing Arien faith and fortitude remains unchanged, even in the face of adversity.

Because "Mars rules," (and Mars is the Roman god of war), Aries is considered by many to be the most physical sign in the Zodiac. A large number of sports figures are born under this sign—including Kareem Adbul-Jabbar, Peyton Manning, Maria Sharapova, Pete Rose, Jennifer Capriati and Secretariat.

Other Ariens of note are Toscanini, Howard Cosell, Aretha Franklin, Vincent van Gogh, Elton John, Carmen Electra, Adolph Hitler, Mariah Carey, Washington Irving, Maya Angelou, Colin Powell, Harry Houdini, Thomas Jefferson and Charlie Chaplin.

Aries is also one of the most highly-charged masculine energy signs in astrology. Aries males are manly men; the females strong, vibrant and forceful. Not necessarily lesbians, you understand, but definitely not frilly and dripping in silk and lace. Denim and leather are more these ladies' style...and they wear it well.

The faint of heart and the easily intimidated are not good matches for an Aries of either sex. It's difficult—and unnatural—for Aries to take the back seat to anything, especially in a relationship. It's understandable how Aries women might find themselves in a quandary in their romantic liaisons. They face the dilemma of needing a "real man" and not a soft Metrosexual, but if they do find a male mighty enough to hold court with them, the two are often at odds over who gets to be on top. It's a slippery slope that the Aries female must learn to master or go it alone.

On the other side of the coin, Aries men need a tough, confident woman (but not too tough!) who can both compliment, deal with (and not wilt under) his strength. Although he is looking for feminine balance to counteract his healthy dose of testosterone, he also needs someone who can stand up to him and not wither in the heat of his fire.

Instead, Aries fellows need a mate who can figure out how to best use his creative, passionate flames to bring out his best qualities. She must be a pretty special gal to keep up with him—white-picket fence quilting homebodies need not apply! Successful relationships must master the perfect (and difficult) balancing act of being an Aries guy's best buddy, his soul mate, his inspiration and the voice of reason. She can't be a pushover yet neither can she push too hard.

Libras, who are always seeking balance, are usually great matches for Aries. So are the other Fire Signs, Leo and Sagittarius—that is if the flames don't run too hot and they don't burn each other out of the kitchen.

Aries is a contradictory and confusing jumble of distinctly male and female components, swirled around in a blender for good measure. Because of the solid male energy that infuses this Sun Sign, female Ariens possess what are considered male traits—they're daring, self-sufficient and naturally spirited. Life with an Aries partner can be many things, but it's certainly never boring. They're also very outspoken and don't sugarcoat anything. So, what you see is what you get.

Aries folks of both sexes are action-oriented. They do rather than say. Impulsivity is also a big component of this Zodiac sign—they tend to act first and ask questions later. Ariens seek—and live—lives that dance on the edge…and they have the battle scars to prove it. But instead of being embarrassed by them, they wear their cuts and bruises proudly, like badges.

Aries Between the Sheets

When you hook up with an Aries, be prepared for a long, hard ride, literally and figuratively. As lovers, they are relentless and have great stamina. To them, sex is a quest and they go at it wholeheartedly, with gusto, until both of you are sore...but in a good way! They truly treat sex like a sport—and not a spectator sport.

Those born under the sign of Aries get off on challenge and the chase. Some may enjoy the pursuit and the conquest even more than the actual act. As with everything else in their lives, the Aries lover knows what they want when they want it and they won't give up (willingly) until they get it. Pursuit is a kind of foreplay for them. If prospective Aries partners are equally aroused by being desired so intensely, it's great. If not, this may cause huge problems. After all, there's a fine line between being pursued and stalked!

Although Aries has the capacity to be very devoted and loving, don't expect hearts and flowers and romance from them, at least not in the traditional sense. For example, when prodded to say, "I love you," a typical Arien response could be, "Of course, I love you...or else I wouldn't be here!" Get used to it. Aries are highly sensual but very cut and dry about what they want—and need.

Like the other barnyard animals in the Zodiac (Capricorn and Taurus), Aries are lusty critters indeed, but moreso for Aries because they have the added bonus of being fueled by the combustibles characteristic of being a Fire Sign. Ariens are most satiated physically when the sex is spontaneous and unrestricted. Wild and uninhibited is their preference.

Remember, as the Sun Sign's Evil Knievels, Aries are game for almost anything. They're known to say that they'll try anything at least once, twice if they really like it. Because of this, it's not uncommon for those born under the sign of Aries to be bisexual, even if it's just occasionally. Dr. Vivian says that whatever your sexual proclivities, don't fight them or judge them. It's best just to go with them. The more you accept your inner desires, the happier you'll be, both in and out of the sack.

I love to tell the story of an Aries friend who found himself in a peep show booth (see, there's that wonderful Arien sense of adventure). When the screen went up, there was a beautiful, bountiful Latina on the other side, who revealed "a Johnson bigger than mine." Instead of being put off by this minor technicality, my buddy made the best of the situation, focused on the bits he liked, and came away with not only a climax, but a hilarious, typically Arien escapade to regale with.

As they do in everyday life, Aries likes to take control in bed. They have an uncanny ability for calling the shots even when they're on the bottom! An Aries man is perfectly content being ridden like a stallion but he somehow manages to take charge with his movements and words even from below—i.e. grabbing his partner's buttocks, urging them on. Likewise, the Aries female is by no means submissive, even when in Missionary position. Beneath her partner, she will move like a liquid fire, hips rising up to meet each thrust.

Although Aries tend to be very aggressive in bed, it's never tinged with violence, just super intense. Again, if you're expecting violins and rose-petals strewn on the sheets, you will be sadly disappointed. But if you crave a spontaneous encounter in an alley that leaves you with your legs trembling, then look no further.

For Aries, their heads are their erogenous zones. They love when you muss their hair or grab their face, and vice versa. It's not uncommon for males to grab a handful of ponytail going down the homestretch. They usually give fantastic head rubs and will be yours forever if you give one in return. And giving or getting "head," well, it goes without saying.

Aries also have extremely sensitive nipples, although many males might be reluctant to admit this, for fear it will make them seem "feminine" and vulnerable. Big, strong Arien males have been known to get rock-hard just from a little nipple play. And it's not uncommon for Arien ladies to have hyper-sensitive nipples. Or to be able to climax solely from having their nipples sucked. It's a sure-fire way to get them moist, at the very least.

Simply put, the Aries mate is also very aroused by their partner's sex organs, so be prepared to be put in the spotlight and have your hotspots worshipped.

Adventurous and outrageous, that's what you can expect from Aries between the sheets. Don't be surprised if they spray-paint their pubes bright green just for fun. Don't expect flowers. But do expect the ride of your life.

The Aries Diet

A Fire Sign through and through, Aries likes it hot—and bold. Complex flavors and tastes are what they crave...and what fuels their daring lifestyles. This is why ethnic cuisines like Mexican, Indian and Thai suit them well, especially dishes like spicy chilis and savory curries.

You are likely to find a wide variety of hot sauces from all over the world in Aries' pantry. Your Arien buddies might even buy a different exotic spice on every vacation. Ditto for chili powders—my guy has selections from New and Old Mexico, India and Arizona, just to name a few. It's not unusual for an Aries to have a heated (what else?) discussion about the virtues and subtle differences between chipotles, habañeros and jalapeños either.

Often excellent cooks, Aries take pride in creating complex, flavorful meals that involve lots of ingredients and chopping. Stews, gumbos, and yes, chili are usually their specialties. Although sometimes their guests will politely bellyache that they're too hot for more subdued palates, Aries efforts in the kitchen are typically successful.

Ariens are also big fans of interactive meals like tacos and fajitas, which require actual work and "building" to eat. Multicourse meals are also favorites. They are in heaven with restaurants' tasting platters and love, love, love buffets —especially in Indian restaurants.

Even with their love of spice, Aries usually has no problem keeping a healthy, balanced diet rich in vegetables like silky *dals* (an Indian lentil dish), *saag paneer* (savory Indian-style spinach) and flavorful beans. They tend to jazz up their spinach and other greens with sautéed garlic, onions — or both.

Recommended for the Aries diet are tomatoes, all varieties of beans, lettuces, cauliflower, cucumber, broccoli, spinach, figs, bananas, apricots and pumpkin. Note that many of these are "watery," like cucumber, which help quench their inner heat.

Related to their Bodypart, many Ariens suffer from headaches and migranes, so if this is the case, caffeine should be limited, or avoided completely. Since they are also prone to head congestion and sinus conditions, dairy products, which can produce excess mucus in people who are intolerant, should be nixed.

But generally speaking, Ariens are pretty hale and hearty beings. Not surprising, the Aries digestive system is especially tolerant of all of this fire and brimstone, and in fact, thrives on it. Only rarely do they suffer from heartburn and when they do, it still doesn't keep them from the flaming foods they yearn for. 'That's what Tums are for,' they will tell you with a wicked grin, 'Right?' Right.

Taurus
April 21 – May 21

Element: Earth

Heavenly Body: Venus

Symbol: The Bull

Stone: Emerald

Lifequest: To feel safe and secure—emotionally and financially

Vibe: Strong and unwavering

Dirty Little Secret: I crave a "white picket fence" kind of life.

Bodyparts: The neck and throat

Fuelfoods: Nothing fancy, please—meat, potatoes and veg...and make sure they don't touch on the plate!

Sign Song: "Ain't No Stopping Us Now"

Movie: *Invincible*—The story of a football player's triumph against all odds represents this astrological bovine's bullish determination.

All About Taurus

Taurus is an extremely puzzling astrological sign. On the outside, they seem perfect. Each hair is in place and they're the epitome of calm, cool and collected. But inwardly, Taureans struggle like crazy to keep up this free and breezy façade. It's so stressful that they are often falling apart inside, and will do almost anything to look like all of their ducks are in a row.

In order to function properly, the Bull needs to be in control—of absolutely everything possible. If not, Taurus very unhappily—and loudly—voices this unhappiness to everyone within earshot. And the strident expression of their misery can carry for blocks. Unkind? Perhaps a little. But my baby sister is a Taurus, so I've had decades of up close and personal experience living with (and loving!) a Taurus.

On the other hand, our fair Dr. Vivian is also a Taurus (with a moon in Libra, thank the heavenly bodies!), and she represents all that is good in this fine Sun Sign. In addition to having control issues, those born under the auspicious sign of Taurus are also practical, patient, kind, reliable, hard-working and competent.

Like the sensible bull that represents this Zodiac sign, Taureans are also determined and well-grounded. In fact, no zodiac sign is closer to the earth than Taurus. This is one reason they love the outdoors so much and dislike being penned in. Many are avid hikers and take to the hills and valleys in all sorts of weather, plodding forward with resolve.

I think it's safe to say that no Sun Sign is as much like its earthly representation than Taurus the Bull. Talk about stubborn! And stubborn doesn't even begin to describe it. The image of butting heads immediately comes to mind—and it's a perfect one for Mr. & Ms. T. Where Aries is resolute, Taurus is downright unmovable. Even when this bull-headed critter is clearly proven wrong, it's almost physically painful for the words "I'm sorry" to pass through their lips.

However, your Taurus buddy will also stick steadfastly by your side when all others have flown the coop and be there beside you through thick and thin. So there is definitely an upside to their tenacity—stubbornness in your favor, so to speak.

Yes, Taurus folks are a diverse and eclectic group and include such notables as Cher, Eva Peron, Bono, William Shakespeare, Adele, Saddam Hussein, Audrey and Katharine Hepburn, Malcolm X, Charlotte Brontë, Yogi Berra, Cate Blanchett, Irving Berlin, Chris Brown, Kirsten Dunst, Duke Ellington, Tina Fey, George Carlin, Golda Meir, Tony Hawk, Bettie Page, Iggy Pop, Jet Li and Shirley Temple. See how different they all are?

Although Taureans have gained the fitting reputation of being socializers, they somehow manage to inconspicuously keep to themselves. They'll let others close but not too close. Definitely not closer than their comfort zone allows. And that invisible force field, that protective layer between them and the outside world, is what makes them feel safe and secure.

Safe and secure are important buzz words for Taurus. They actually crave—and need—what I call a "white picket fence" life to feel tranquil and fulfilled. Now, this doesn't mean that Taureans must be in a straight, traditional male/female relationship in order to be serene, but even in a same-sex union, they need the steady partner, the stable home and financial stability. Happy, healthy and wealthy are three things they strive for. If all of the above aren't in place, then Taurus feels—and acts—terribly off balance.

Remember that adorable book, *The Story of Ferdinand*, when you were a kid? All Ferdie the Bull wanted to do was to sit in the pasture under his favorite cork tree and sniff flowers. He didn't want to chase after matadors and their red capes. But when pushed—in Ferdinand's case, it was by a bee sting—he went berserk. To me, this story is a perfect illustration of the Taurean temperament.

Taurus has a very clear idea of the way things *should* be. Not only don't they want the comfortable applecart of their existence to get upset, but they have a definite image of the way each and every apple on that cart should be arranged. It can sometimes be frustrating trying to work with (or doing a chore for) a Taurus because it's difficult to get it right—right being the way they do things. Which, in their eyes, is the only way!

Many wrongly judge the Taurus as being arrogant, inhibited, dull, or even moody, but this simply isn't the case. Their true shining spirits are lurking just beneath the surface, perhaps obscured by the thin veil of routine chores.

Diligent and dependable, Taurus is one you want as your attorney, accountant or in charge of your construction job site, because not only will they get the job done, but they get the job done efficiently. You can trust a Taurean to do it quickly, cheaply and thoroughly—and then some.

Even though Taurus has their feet planted firmly on the ground, and rarely, if ever, loses their footing, they have a difficult time letting go and truly relaxing. But it's fine with them. They are happiest when life is *status quo* and things go sailing merrily along without any bumps in the road or surprises. It's almost as though they work (and work very well, thank you!)

on their personal brand of automatic pilot, deftly turning off outside distractions.

Taurus is a "feel good" Sun Sign, hardwired to seek life's comforts even when their finances don't match their sumptuous desires. I have a Taurean friend who will savor every luscious sip of their $6 latte and happily forgo lunch in order to afford that luxury. My philosophy is more power to ya. If that's what gives you joy and is true to your Sun Sign, then it's better to go with what comes naturally than to fight it and be miserable.

Change isn't a word those born under the Taurus sun like—or do well with. But to their credit, when confronted with Plan B, Taureans do their best to adapt, establish that new pattern and stick with it as long as humanly possible. Until the next time the stars send them into a tailspin.

A lifelong (and fruitless!) quest of theirs is to plan things out in advance. I paraphrase what the ever poetic Bobby Burns once said about the best laid plans of mice and men...they often go awry. And this is so difficult for Taureans to accept. Although, to their credit, they do try.

A Taurus also likes to always be of use. This makes them susceptible to becoming "helicopter parents." You know the type, always hovering above their kids, trying to do everything for them, even when they are into their 20s and should be on their own. Letting go is an eternal Taurean struggle, whether it be their children, a relationship that has long gone sour or dealing with a death.

Worry warts extraordinaire, Taurus are easily prone to being nervous and anxious, especially when confronted with that dreaded "C word"—change. Extremely sensitive, they are skilled at hiding their feelings and their vulnerability, but deep inside, they take everything to heart.

As friends go, Taurus folks make the best buddies. They treat friends like family, and cherished family members at that. Loyal and dependable, like a faithful canine, Taureans are always there when you need them...but they like to lead you on the leash, and not the other way around.

Taurus Between the Sheets

The Taurean tug-of-war with change and their need for sameness explains their legendary lack of spontaneity in the bedroom. Although the Taurus mate is very adept at lovemaking, they also like to be prepared, to be "ready." And sometimes lovin' just don't play that way!

Taurus likes advance warning before a romantic liaison so they can take a shower, shave and put on something nice and get in the mood. If you can deal with pretty much making an appointment for sex, then you're in for an enjoyable evening. Just so long as you arrive at the designated time.

Some might call erotic encounters with a Taurus "vanilla" — but it's the best, creamiest, most delicious brand of vanilla in your grocery store's freezer section. Taureans are highly physical partners with a very distinct idea of what sex should be.

For example, Taurus is most comfortable when bedroom bombastics have a defined beginning, middle and an end. And they don't take kindly to, say, skipping foreplay for an impromptu romp in the laundry room. Most Taureans just can't get their heads around the concept of a quickie! However, if you can handle pre-planned nookie then you're likely to find them to be satisfying in the sack.

But for Bulls, sex is no-frills and down to business all the way. Which explains the way my Taurus friend describes her torrid encounters. When Liz gets to the naughty bits, she always says, "Then we did what we had to do…" And I think, 'Really???' How can you refer to something as amazing and mind-blowing as sex like it's a simple bodily function akin to blowing your nose or using the toilet? But that's the difference between a Taurus and the Libra. It's a battle of practical vs. sensual.

Although their' ruling planet is Venus, Taurus is not unabashedly erotic in the same way as Libra, who's also ruled by Venus, is. With Taurus, you have a potential hottie but a hottie who is always reigning themselves in. Taureans do let themselves go…but only so far. Good matches are Scorpio, the sometimes fussy Virgo and the equally-steadfast Capricorn.

One-night-stands also aren't in the Taurus vocabulary. These are far too random for their liking. As you might expect, this Sun Sign does best with regular sex partners. That's when they can let down their guards, well, as much as this is possible for a Taurus to do. Abstinence is especially difficult for Taureans, again, because it disturbs the regular flow of *the way things should be*.

In a Taurus lover, you get someone who is faithful and true but also really jealous, often irrationally so. It's not unusual for them to smell their husband's Johnson for evidence of infidelity when the unsuspecting gent comes home late from work. (I'm serious!) And then they're completely satisfied when they get a clean reading—as though they never heard of soap and water to erase any sign of philandering.

The neck and throat are major erogenous zones for the benevolent Bull. A deep tissue neck rub will make them yours forever. They just melt for kisses up and down their throats, including playful nibbles and deep love bites—sometimes hard enough to leave marks. Taureans wear hickies proudly, like jewelry.

Males born under this sign have lots of erotic endurance and can go on forever, like a good breeding bull. Taurus ladies are often multi-orgasmic but very pragmatic and systematic about how they get there. For example, you have to move your tongue or hips just so, no deviation from the theme. Touch and smell are extremely important to the Taurean's ultimate pleasure. And yours!

The Taurus Diet

It stands to reason that the Sun Sign who likes nothing fancy between the sheets and prefers a conventional, carefully plotted-out life would also have simple, no-nonsense tastes when it comes to the kitchen.

Taureans are famously predictable eaters. Nothing fancy, just equal helpings of meat, potatoes and vegetables—and make sure nothing's touching on the plate. No exotic veggies like sweet and sour Brussel sprouts or candied kale. Plain white or maybe brown rice (if they're in a cheeky mood) but definitely not wild rice. And don't try to sneak fingerlings, Yukon gold or (gasp!) purple spuds into a side dish. Straight-up Idaho potatoes will do them just fine.

Taureans are the ones who will order the same things in the same restaurant the same way—they look forward to it. They're cool with roasted chicken even when there's succulently crispy duck on the menu. Taureans are also content with having the same thing for breakfast, lunch and dinner every day. They're the folks who walk into the corner diner and say, "The usual," because for Taurus the usual is the best.

Other faves: Robust, thick cuts of beef suit this Bull well. And well done, at that.

Because Taurus folks have notoriously slow metabolisms, they have to work hard to stay in shape and not gain weight. But they also enjoy the predictable routine of working out at the gym—and generally have their favorite machines, so heavens help anyone who's on their StairMaster. The good news is that Taurus' diligent and patient nature meshes nicely with the rigors of being a gym rat and carrying out a serious diet program.

Dr. Ray warns Taureans to pay strict attention to keeping a balanced diet and to limit fat, sugar and starch intake to keep the battle of the bulge at bay. Good, healthy foods that this Sun Sign processes well are asparagus, beets, cauliflower, spinach, cucumbers, onions, pumpkins, all types of raw nuts and cranberries. Although they don't need to be complete vegans, limiting their intake of the complex proteins they naturally crave (like meat) can work to their advantage. Think simple, whole grains, much like a bull eats, at least for breakfast, to give the day a good, balanced start. Hot oatmeal, farro and cream of wheat are all good breakfast bets.

Since throat problems often plague Taurus, special care should be taken to keep the thyroid functioning at its utmost. Foods filled with natural iodine like fish and seafood should also be eaten, at least occasionally. Other healthy bets are eggs, liver, kidney beans, wheat germ, fresh fruit and green salads. Processed carbs and heavy, rich foods should be avoided.

Gemini
May 22 – June 211

Element: Air

Heavenly Body: Mercury

Symbol: The Twins

Stone: Aquamarine

Lifequest: To sample it all

Vibe: Quivers with intelligence

Dirty Little Secret: I have to do it, see it, experience it before anyone else does.

Bodypart: The shoulders

Fuelfoods: Favors a diverse palate, international cuisines, smorgasbords and finger foods

Sign Song: "Two Hearts"

Movie: *Twins*—Though delightfully goofy, this flick, which pits Danny DeVito and Arnold Schwarzenegger as twins separated at birth, will strike a chord with Zodiac's Twins.

All About Gemini

Maybe I should start with a disclaimer and say that no two Gemini are alike. This is because of the duality of the Sun Sign, the Twins. Like the other "two part" signs—Libra and Pisces—Gems are constantly seeking balance and steadiness. But instead of two fish or two balancing scales, Gemini has the added complication of having two whole people in their stars. And these Twins, on their quest for equilibrium, sometimes fight each other like relentless warriors.

That being said, it's not unusual to know Gemini who are at totally opposite ends of the spectrum. They're a very difficult sign to pin down! One Gem friend might be outgoing and boisterous, while another is shy, withdrawn and quick to blush.

This Sun Sign is ruled by the shoulders, but its mastery often extends to the hands, arms and even the fingers. You'll note that Gemini is able to "shoulder" a great deal of responsibility and also, to bear heavy loads (literally and figuratively) that other astrological signs cannot. Because of this strength, it's hard for Gemini to ask for help, even if a situation is crippling them. Somehow, somewhere, they gain the tenacity to carry on—from their other Twin, perhaps?

It's tough to keep up with a Gemini, because they always seem to be in motion, flitting from one activity to the next. Remember Mercury, Roman mythology's fleet-footed messenger of the gods? He was always on the run, shooting back and forth across the heavens with his jaunty winged helmet with matching footwear to propel him. Since Mercury is Gemini's ruling planet, this explains the sign's wanderlust.

Astrology's Twins also have a hunger to learn and a thirst for fresh experiences. Because of this, they are often voracious readers, commonly plowing through several books on different subjects simultaneously. They see the world as their buffet and they want to sample every bit of it—and before anyone else does. Competitive? Sure, but not in the same way as Aries is.

Gems want to inhale life because of an innate desire to see, feel and taste, not to get a leg up on anyone else. To Gemini, it's all about the experience. They don't give a hoot about what the Joneses are up to, but they're more than happy to have company if the J's want to come along for the ride.

Naturally inquisitive, Gemini has also gotten the bad rap of being a wee bit naughty. They like to wreak gentle havoc, mix two combustible materials in a beaker, step back and see what happens. However, it's not meanness which provokes this type of behavior, just a healthy curiosity about the world around them.

Yes, Gemini are the mischievous imps of the Zodiac. As kids, they're the ones most likely to do "ring and runs" throughout the neighborhood or put two cats in a cardboard box just "to see what happens."

Gemini are also Jacks and Jills of All Trades but Masters of None. True to the duplicity of the sign, they are usually multitalented as well as multi-dimentional. Think of them as amazing jewels with all of these wonderful facets carved into their surfaces, and every time you look at them, you notice something different.

In addition, Geminis have managed to nab the title of the "Chatty Cathys" of the Zodiac. Some might go as far as to call them big yappers or incessant talkers but I beg to differ here. Their talk is not idle or without merit. Gems are usually wonderful conversationalists and can keep you riveted for hours. They are blessed with the gift of gab. Unlimited talk and text plans are a must for this Sun Sign. Gemini can charm the stripes off a zebra, and then some!

The Twins do have a love affair with words — and words love them back. If a Gemini isn't oratorically-gifted, then they usually have an up close and personal relationship with words. There are many skilled writers among their ranks as well as folks who speak a variety of languages. And don't forget librarians!

Well known Gemini include Bob Dylan, Queen Victoria, Rosemary Clooney, John F. Kennedy, Marilyn Monroe, Josephine Baker, Allan Ginsberg, Joe Namath, Paul Gauguin, Judy Garland, Jacques Cousteau, Gene Wilder, Anne Frank, Boy George, Nicole Kidman, Maurice Sendak, Salman Rushdie, Paula Abdul, Johnny Depp, and Donald Trump. See what I mean? A common denominator for most on this list is words, be it singing, public speaking, performing or coming up with a catchphrase like "You're fired!"

In lifepartners, Gemini look for someone who can keep up with their frenetic pace physically and mentally. Usually, it's a person who doesn't mind taking a backseat to their spotlight-seeking –and achieving — mate. Successful pairings include Libra, Aquarius and sometimes Leo.

Although Gemini is an Air Sign, they are not flighty as some astrologers claim. I prefer the descriptors of changeable, unpredictable and eccentric. True, Gems are cerebral but they also tend to be like a strong, sudden gust: picking up anything in its path, moving erratically from one place to another, never slowing down.

Gemini generally lead dynamic and exciting lives. Like it or not, they're the ones people talk about, good or bad. Most astrologists would agree that along with Scorpio and Virgo, Gemini is one of the "most discussed" Sun Signs. Not only that but they're often dissected and sometimes even criticized.

Why? Jealousy, perhaps. You can't be so "out there," so front-and-center and in the spotlight without ruffling a few envious feathers. I'd go so far as to say that Gemini are commonly misunderstood and even unappreciated for their talents, which might be overshadowed by their larger-than-life personalities.

Gemini's duplicitous nature can extend to money matters. Some are very good at making—and spending—money and tend to be shrewd investors. These Gems might gravitate toward the stock market or investment banking.

Other Gems are extremely bad at handling finances, end up in bankruptcy court or somehow find themselves with large, unruly credit card bills. Their wild abandon with wampum could lead them to make some very daring, but ultimately some very devastating, business choices. Gemini are often on the precipice of financial ruin but like cats, can quickly land on their feet and recover. They see this as incredibly exciting but it can drive their partners (or their relationships) to an early grave.

It's not surprising that Gemini love games. They're attracted to anything that involves deep thought and out-maneuvering their opponents mentally. You'll never win against them in Tic-Tac-Toe. And forget about chess!

Gemini Between the Sheets

Remember what I said about Gemini and words? Well, it carries into the bedroom. Dr. Vivian reports that many of her clients born under this extremely oral sign of the Zodiac claim that they can literally be talked to orgasm—or that they can chat their partners to nirvana.

Gemini are dirtytalkers supreme and have been known to elevate it to an art form. They're so good at it that it's difficult for partners to compete but Gemini will appreciate your efforts to keep up, even if your pornographic prose is nowhere near as creative or downright nasty as theirs is. Filthy philosophizing just seems to effortlessly spill from between their lips. In fact, after the heat of the moment, they're apt to be a little embarrassed about what they said.

And speaking of lips, Gemini tend to very gifted at kissing. They will treat lovers to twists of the tongue they never imagined. Liplock with The Twins is guaranteed to curl your toes, straighten your hair and tie your knickers in a bow.

Gemini are also very skilled in oral sex. They're so fantastic at it that you might think they have two tongues. In a sense, they do. Not only are Gems artful at cunnilingus and fellatio, but they supremely enjoy performing the act. So much so that they might actually prefer giving head a bit more than getting it. Don't be insulted if your Gemini partner would rather give than receive—it's just in their nature, so just go with it. Believe it or not, they get off on you getting off almost as much as you do!

Be prepared for a very enjoyable romp when you bed a Gemini. Their lovemaking is varied, energetic and creative. They're curious about all kinds of sexual expression and are usually game for anything and are willing to try out something new. This is one reason they're comfortable and confident in threesomes, especially trios which include two same-sex partners—again, due to the Twin aspect of their Sun Sign.

Role-playing games can be extremely fulfilling with a Gemini—they are imaginative and fun-loving—but be sure that the scenarios are varied. Gems are easily bored with the same old, same old scenario, even in fantasy. Keep a storehouse of ideas, props and costumes on hand for any role-playing forays with The Twins. They can only reinact "The Cheerleader and the Football Star" so many times before wanting to branch off into "The Headmaster and the Naughty Student." And one guess who likes to be the top!

A downside to Gemini's "oral fixation" might be their tendency to break out into a lengthy treatise in the middle of sex. To them, talk is just extended foreplay—it turns them on. But no worries, they're easily redirected. Sometimes a hard, passionate kiss on the mouth is all it takes to shut them up and get your point across.

Some Gemini are sexually promiscuous, flitting from partner to partner like a bumblebee from flower to flower. (That's one of the reasons they're known as the butterflies of the Zodiac!) Others prefer one partner and have A LOT of sex with them. But this has less to do with actual horniness and more to do with the Gemini desire to do it all.

Although Gems are sensual individuals, they're generally more driven by their intellect than by their desires. Some may even overthink sex to the point of distraction so that it disturbs their enjoyment of the act. Their hyperactive mind might be so pronounced that it interferes with a man's ability to sustain an erection and with a woman's capacity to climax. Remedying the situation could simply be an instance of mind over matter, but if the impotence persists, seeking the advice of a professional like Vivian is strongly advised.

However, in most cases, the Gemini tendency to constantly examine the "what if's" and "buts" in life doesn't sneak into the bedroom. With a Gemini, you are practically guaranteed an attentive, playful lover worthy of a trophy for Oral Excellence.

The Gemini Diet

Gemini's approach to life as a smorgasbord that begs to be sampled, savored and enjoyed extends to the dining room table. Gems are adventurous eaters, to say the least. They'll be the first in the group to sample chocolate-covered ants and crackly chili-fried crickets. They don't turn up their noses at oddly-colored foods. Bring on the bright blue potato chips and dusky black squid ink pasta. With a side dish of garlicky octopus, even better.

Novelty foods are a favorite, including green bagels for St. Patrick's Day (even if they aren't Irish), pigs in a blanket and finger foods, too. At a dim sum restaurant, they'll eat first and ask questions later, be it jellyfish, chicken feet or frogs' legs. Cute foods like intricately carved hors d'oeuvres and complicated sushi are also faves.

Gemini thinks nothing of mixing cultures—and all on one plate. This is why the buffet table and all-you-can-eat restaurants are favorite dining choices of theirs. It doesn't have to be fancy, there just have to plenty of selections and plenty of food.

Call Gems international eaters. They would happily munch themselves across the globe, happily devouring the best of what each culture has to offer, then come back for seconds. It's hard to predict what a Gemini might order in a restaurant but a good bet would be the Daily Special or a dish that's not even on the menu.

Many Gemini can't tolerate large amounts of food at one sitting—although they do try—so it's best for them to eat mini meals throughout the day. This is one reason they have the reputation of being grazers. They are also especially sensitive to caffeine and other stimulants, so these should be consumed in moderation.

As you might imagine, Gemini has a tendency to overindulge, so this carries into their love of food and drink. A large proportion of this Sun Sign is overweight and/or heavy drinkers, so care must be taken in these areas. Moderation isn't a word usually associated with these over-the-top Twins, but Ray encourages Gems to make an effort not to overdo it at the table or the bar.

It also isn't tough to believe that Gemini are prone to delicate stomachs and digestive issues but this is more due to their over-indulging rather than having tender bellies like Aries does.

Raw foods don't go down easily for Gemini, which is why they skip the salad bar at the buffet. Good food choices for this Sun Sign include greens like asparagus, spinach and green beans and fruits and veggies high in beta-carotene like tomatoes, carrots, oranges, peaches and apricots.

Cancer/Moon Child
June 22 – July 23

Element: Water

Heavenly Body: The Moon

Symbol: The Crab

Stone: Moonstone

Lifequest: To feel treasured, connected and cherished

Vibe: More changeable than the tide

Dirty Little Secret: I have an intense need to feel secure in all aspects of my life—in bed, in the soul, in the pocketbook.

Bodyparts: The stomach and breasts

Fuelfoods: Predictable comfort foods—like Momma's meat loaf and hearty soups—rule

Sign Song: "Fly Me to the Moon"

Movie: *Tell Me That You Love Me, Junie Moon*–Otto Preminger's wild romp (a precursor to *One Flew Over the Cuckoo's Nest*) captures the Moon Child's desire to be adored.

All About Moon Child

First of all, I've always taken offense to the very auspicious Sun Sign name "Cancer"—it seems doomed from the get-go. I prefer "Moon Child," which is more of a mouthful, but has much nicer connotations. But because of the negatives from The Big C, I'll use abbreviations throughout—either C or MC—and also call them Lunarians. Please bear with me but I just feel this will help Mooners get over the rap some have given them as the Zodiac's badasses.

Where no two Gemini are alike, MCs can go through a slew of personality changes all in one day. To say that this Sun Sign is an enigma is a vast understatement. They are a pileup of contradictions on this highway we call life. One minute they're sweet, the next jealous, then caring and a millisecond later, they can cut deep with a biting remark. Describing MCs as moody doesn't even begin to tell their story.

One reason Lunarians are so unpredictable is because, as their name implies, they're guided by the moon. As you know, the moon is slightly different each day as it melts from full to new phases, then beefs up again. Another reason for their volatility is because their ruling element is water, an even more changeable element. Water can either conform to the space that holds it or overflow its boundaries in a raging flood. Water can nourish but it can also destroy.

This Zodiac sign is symbolized by the crab, which is another bundle of contradictions. Crabs are hard as rocks on the outside, but penetrate that tough layer and they're soft and susceptible on the inside. And forget about when they're molting and shed their shells altogether! In addition, crabs are quick to retreat into their shells at the slightest provocation.

Talk about vulnerable! The seafood lovers among you also know that although crabs are delicious, they are oh so difficult to eat—but well worth the effort. (More about challenges to penetrate their "inner crab" in the "Between the Sheets" section.) So too MCs are well worth the effort of getting to know. It just takes a lot of hard work—and sometimes, a little mallet.

Once you get past the Crab's thorny layers, you're rewarded with a depth of sensitivity and kindness that makes C's so exceptional. Be forewarned that you just might get pinched a few times by their sharp pincers!

Life is a whirlwind for MCs. Even if they're standing there minding their own business, trouble seems to find them. That's because of their strong ties to the moon which greatly affects their own personal seas of emotion. C's affinity with the moon can also make it difficult for them to function at a constant level each day. Their feelings are on a continuous see-saw ride, dragging them—and anyone else in their lives—along with it. Much like an undertow in an otherwise calm sea.

But the wild-card life of a Moonie is also part of their charm. Just like that big box of chocolates, you never know what you're gonna get. While most find this maddening, still others, like Pisces and Taurus, are junkies to the excitement. However, sparks can fly with Gemini and Aries.

A handful of well-known MCs are Bill Cosby, Edward Hopper, Helen Keller, Cyndi Lauper, P.T. Barnum, Ernest Hemingway, Pamela Anderson, Tom Hanks, Nikola Tesla, Kevin Bacon, Ringo Starr, Liv Tyler, Freddie Prinze, Carly Simon,

Nelson and John Rockefeller, Peter Paul Rubens, Courtney Love and Michael Phelps. A formidable list, to say the least.

Tread lightly with the Moon Child. Critics say they're willful, stubborn and used to getting their way. (Remember those sharp pincers!) But I like to point out that they are also passionate, careful, kind and generous. True, MCs are known to retreat into their shells but they're also famous for striking out when things don't go their way. Some might even venture that MCs can be a wee bit spiteful. Their long and strong memories don't generally allow them to forgive and forget. Forgive, maybe after a time, but they're the elephants of the Zodiac—they never forget a thing!

The two most important things to a MC are love and romance and not necessarily in that order. Having lots of money in the bank (i.e. security) is a close third. They are notoriously gifted at nookie and will charm the boxers and bloomers off their intended. When C's are deep in lust, nothing else matters but when good lovin' goes bad, watch out. Nobody feels a broken heart quite so profoundly as a MC. Just as they are prone to soaring high, they also fall hard from those dizzying heights.

For Moon Children, it's all about the home, but that's not to say they're homebodies. They're big on the importance of family and upholding tradition. Moonies often come from, or have, large families. The more the merrier is their motto. MCs are also extremely nurturing and will be among the first to offer a helping hand when someone's in a bind.

It's been said that Lunarians are the first to laugh, the first to cry—and it's often one after the other. Crabs are also purported to be lazy, but I don't agree. Although they often need a push or a motivator, once they get started, there's no stopping them.

Because the stomach is their ruling Bodypart, an MC who "goes with their gut" can expect smooth sailing. Problems start when they fight their natural instincts and use other means to steer their destinies.

Overall, these children of the Moon are captivating, mysterious, exciting and alluring. Combine this with their nurturing spirit and you've got the makings of a fine Sun Sign. As long as they feel safe and secure—and are consistently reassured—the pull of their needy tides will stay at bay and it will be smooth sailing.

Moon Child Between the Sheets

Despite their tough exterior, Moon Children tend to be extraordinarily attentive lovers, thoroughly kind and thoughtful. Goes with the nurturing territory. They're also extremely romantic—when they're not being distant and moody. But it's usually easy to lure this critter out of its shell either by giving them time and space to come out on their own or by showering them with a healthy dose of TLC.

Perhaps it's due to their propensity for change but MCs are into role-playing, as long as the games are edgy. They favor slave scenarios and prefer to be the bottom. It's usually okay to be a wee bit mean and even aggressive to Cs during gametime— but Dr. Vivian stresses that it's important to lay down the ground rules first.

However, even in Master/slave play, Lunarians need to know that they're loved and cherished. They need constant reassurance and if they don't get it, they are likely to stray until they find it.

For some reason, the Moon Child's erotic proclivities always remind me of Florence and the Machine's song "Kiss with a Fist"—but not enough to name it as its Sign Song. It's a playfully violent look into an odd dom/dom relationship that works. Break the lock if it don't fit!

MC's tend to prefer sexual postures that most others find downright uncomfortable. A favorite is lying on the side with one lover curled behind the other's back—crablike, if you will. This works especially well for vaginal as well as anal sex and gives open access to the chest as well as to the genitals.

Moonies are notorious for being the Sun Sign that's extremely attracted to breasts. It's one (or two!) of their ruling Bodyparts. MC men can zoom in on this feature and nothing else while MC gals love drawing attention to their cleavage in daringly low cut blouses, naughty bras, or even better yet, no bras at all. The flesh of their breasts (not so much the nipples) are especially sensitive to finger and tongue stimulation. MC men like to bring focus to this area of their anatomy as well and will often shave their chests to heighten their sensitivity and visibility.

Another of this Sun Sign's erogenous zones is the stomach. Not very sexy, you think? Well, to an MC it is! I know of several MC men whose ropes rise just from a little tummy tickling. For real. One confessed to Dr. V that he had difficulty reaching an orgasm unless his stomach was stimulated as well as his penis.

Moonie ladies often have prominent bellies. Not potbellies, but cute little poochies. Remember that scene from *Pulp Fiction* where the adorable Fabienne extols the virtues of "having a bit of a tummy...like Madonna when she did 'Lucky Star'..." Dollars to donuts Fabienne was a MC. And she was right, pots can be cute.

I mentioned earlier that Crabs are sometimes known as the Bad Boys (and Girls) of the Zodiac. With all of that nurturing and emphasis on hearth and home, they're not the most faithful Sun Sign under the sun. They can probably give a pretty convincing argument about why it's a good idea to have an affair with them—even if you're perfectly happy with your mate. You might actually find yourself seriously considering their proposition, if not succumbing to their charms.

However, this brand of "Runaround Sue" behavior might have more to do with their insecurities and less to do with actual desire, Dr. V says. To keep a Lunarian in one bed (yours!) it's important that they are constantly reassured that they're appreciated. A partner who's constantly criticizing or berating them—like a Taurus might—has a good chance of chasing a MC from their boudoir into someone else's.

Due to their elusive nature, Moon Children won't always verbalize their sexual desires to their partners. Knowing what turns on a MC mate might be somewhat of a mystery, but it's guaranteed that you will have a great time trying to find out! And be rewarded with a caring and comforting paramour in return.

The Moon Child Diet

Comfort foods rule for MC's. Thick, robust soups. Creamy macaroni and cheese. Crusty meatloaf—with a hard-boiled egg and/or molten cheese tucked inside, even better. Trays of dense, delicious lasagna. Yummy French onion soup. You get the idea. Hot, hearty and gooey.

And if you see a pattern of cheesy goodness here, you're absolutely right. Many Sun Signs (like Aries) would be running for their stash of little purple pills with such a diet but for Lunarians, digesting dairy and protein-heavy meals is no problem.

Remember, the stomach is one of their ruling organs—and it's generally very strong in MCs. If a Moonie does have a weak digestive system, it can usually be blamed on stress and anxiety, which sends them into a tailspin more pronounced than it does other Sun Signs.

Ray says that fresh veggies, fresh fruit and lean proteins should be on any C's daily "to eat" lists so they can avoid icks like receding gums and eye problems, which many MCs are prone to. Other good news foods for C's are egg yolks, whole grains like rye, yogurt, beets, fish and oysters. They should steer clear of starches, sugar and salt as much as possible. Ditto for hot peppery sauces and anything containing horseradish, which wreak havoc on their normally steady digestive systems.

Although they couldn't be called gourmets, MCs are usually whiz kids when it comes to creating simple, stick-to-the-ribs foods. Give them a package of pork chops, an onion, a potato and a bottle of ketchup and they can come up with a delicious feast. A hearty picnic at the beach, with a big selection of "old standard" salads like macaroni, potato and three bean is their idea of heaven. MCs often have a repertoire of "five easy pieces"—a quintet of dishes they know how to prepare really well—which make an impression on dates and in-laws alike.

As youngsters, Moonies are usually blessed with very fast metabolisms but in later years, when things slow down a bit, they can be prone to weight gain. But as long as they avoid sweets and refined sugars and starches, MCs should be able to keep the scales in check.

The nutrition newsflash is that Moon Children are notoriously easy to please in the kitchen just so long as you KIS—keep it simple.

Leo
July 24 – August 23

Element: Fire

Heavenly Body: The Sun

Symbol: The Lion

Stone: Peridot

Lifequest: To lead—and be loyally followed

Vibe: Glows with power

Dirty Little Secret: I think I'm king (or queen) of the jungle, therefore I am.

Bodypart: The heart and the spine

Fuelfoods: Meat, meat and more meat! The bloodier the better.

Sign Song: "You Gotta Have Heart"

Movie: *Braveheart*—This epic which portrays how one man's quest for freedom amid adversity changes the destiny of an entire people is demonstrative of this Lion's tenacity and strength.

All About Leo

"Leo the Lionhearted"—that's all you need to know about the fifth sign of the Zodiac. Just like this star feline rules the heavens, so too must it rule everything within its kingdom to keep propelling itself forward on an even kilter. True, the Lion can be a ferocious, blustery monarch but it can also be kind, beneficent and just. And more often than not, it is. Leos are traditionally extremely good leaders and quite rightly, have a loyal entourage of followers.

Magnetic, charming and progressive, not only do Leos draw an overflow of friends but they also attract oodles of opportunities. Like any cat, these Lions always manage to land on their feet, even amid a storm of adversity—and they do it with panache and a proverbially sunny attitude. After all, these warriors are ruled by the sun, the brightest star in our skies.

Leo expects—and gets—nothing less: to be the brightest star on everyone's horizon. There's no bones about it, they simply need to be King of the Hill and Queen of the Hop. And who's to argue? These leonine creatures consistently outshine the competition with very little effort on their part. Their natural spark and *joie de vivre* always shine through.

Leo is indeed a lucky sign because it seems that the very heavens have smiled down upon it. And even when this Lion makes bad decisions, things still seem to go well—or at least not as awfully as they could. Some of this has to do with the positive vibes Leo always shines forth, even in the face of misfortune. And some of it is just plain dumb luck.

Along with Aries and Sagittarius, Leo is one of Zodiac's three Fire Signs but our stellar Lion is very different than each of his flaming filial companions. While Aries' fire is explosive and Sagittarius' is unrestrained, this Sun Sign's flame can best be described as a slow burn. It's the fire that keeps you warm, the fire that cooks your food, the fire does no harm if kept in check.

So too does Leo's heartfire rule because this Sun Sign is guided by its large, lovely heart. Love conquers all for the solar Lion. Leo's heart is its great motivator. The heart is what helps it make all of its decisions in life and in love. While Cancer goes from the gut, with Leo, the fist-sized muscle in the center of its chest guides it.

The spine is Leo's secondary ruling Bodypart and the Lion's backbone is like iron. Because of this, they tend to be fine dancers and gifted athletes. Problems arise, however, when Leos push themselves too hard and tax their usually-strong muscles.

Generally speaking, Zodiac's Lions are blessed with endurance and tend to live long, healthy lives. But many don't know when to slow down and take a breather, taxing their powerful hearts, sometimes making them susceptible to problems in this area. (More heart warnings in the "Diet" section.)

Once a Leo is committed to a relationship and declares ownership, they are devoted 110% and faithful almost to a flaw. If their tender emotions or faith is ever broken, that's it. No amount of tears or apologies can ever win them back. When a business or personal relationship ends, even one decades in the making, it is over. Leos can leave it behind without turning back even once. They can sever ties as deeply and irrevocably as cutting an artery.

But Leos never end relationships without due cause. There's always a solid reason (often several) for them to call it quits. For Lions, when it's over, it's over. Forever. Not only has the fat lady sung but she's left the building. However, if you've got the love of a Leo, it's also yours for an eternity.

This Sun Sign makes wheels turn. They make things happen. They are society's innovators, they are movers and shakers. It's obvious to all around them that they're leaders, even to other leaders. Among well-known Leos are Napoleon Bonaparte, Amelia Earhart, Neil Armstrong, Tony Bennett, Jennifer Lopez, Dustin Hoffman, Martha Stewart, Ben Affleck, Percy Bysshe Shelley, Halle Berry, Sean Penn, Haile Selassie, Julia Child, Robert DeNiro, Mae West, Slash, Dorothy Hamill, Cecil B. DeMille, Robert Plant, Lucille Ball, James Baldwin, JK Rowling, Alfred Hitchcock, Robert Redford, Andy Warhol and Louis Armstrong. Lions all!

Leo's one fault—and it's a biggie—is pride. Closely followed by flattery, which is their Achilles heel. In fact, the old adage, "Flattery will get you everywhere" could be Leo's mantra. The stars' Lion is a tad self-righteous and overconfident, even when they have a right to puff out their chests. Their head gets a bit too swelled for their own good, and often clouds their judgment.

The other side of the proud coin is that Leos simply cannot deal with criticism of any kind, even sugar-coated or constructive. Critiquing a Lion is a sure-fire way to end the association. They crave approval and crumble at the tiniest bit of rejection.

Most astrologists adhere to the belief that there are three distinct types of Leos:

> • **Sphinx** – This is the most sophisticated level, depicted by a lone creature bestowed with great wisdom and teaching abilities

> • **Lion** – A jungle king (or queen) moved mostly by ego but always protective of its tribe; and

> • **Cub** – Not fully developed, they cower from new experiences, stick to a momma-figure like glue and can't stand to be away from the pride.

Dedicated and true, Leos make excellent partners if you are willing to step aside and be led by one of the ablest bodies in astrology. Suggested mates for these Lions include Aquarius, which is at the opposite end of the Zodiac, but has complimentary qualities. Aries and Sagittarius are generally also good matches.

Leo Between the Sheets

Just like Leo quests to be the top in all aspects of their life, so too do they strive to be the leader in the bedroom. Although they (almost) always need to be the aggressor and initiate erotic liaisons, Lions are also determined, committed lovers. In other words, it ain't over until everybody's satisfied. The heavens' lusty leonine looks after the entire pride, even if it's just a pride of one, meaning their significant other.

This is not to say that Leo doesn't also have a healthy sense of "me time" between the sheets. Role-playing scenarios for them focus on love, devotion and being the center of attention. Being catered to is a front-and-center reoccurring fantasy. A lord or lady serviced by an underling, in any and every method possible, is a sure-fire way to ignite their lust. Imagine a king or queen seated at the throne, their crouching subject on hands and knees perched between the monarch's spread thighs, pleasuring them with their mouth. You get the picture!

In the sack, Leos prefer dominant erotic postures—anything that makes them feel like they're in charge. For men, it's missionary and for the ladies, it's cowgirl (woman on top). Both sexes are partial to rear-entry positions, commonly known as doggie-style, where both partners are on their knees. Nothing makes a man feel like a king or makes a lady feel more like a naughty kitten!

Although Leo is most aroused when they're treated like the gods and goddesses they truly are, they're not above reversing roles every now and again, to get a taste for how the other half lives and loves. After all, in their eyes, giving another being pleasure, making them quiver and shiver in orgasm, is a sort of mastery all in itself.

Since self-pride is a strong motivator for Leos, they tend to be excellent lovers. These lions have to be the best at everything, including lovemaking. They need to shine, even when giving, and that's good news for Leo's sex partners.

The downside is that Leos can be incredibly possessive, jealous and insecure. They're not above lying to impress their mates—or to secure their devotion. In Leo's case, it's a desperation move that they'll only resort to when feeling cornered. Leos are simply not cheaters and they don't lie to pull one over on their mates. If they do spout falsehoods, it's only to secure love.

To avoid this silly brand of game-playing, be sure to tell your Leo how wonderful they are and how much they're appreciated. A lot. This will keep their egos sufficiently pumped up but not to the degree that they're out of control.

Leo is also unique in that they can't seem to separate love from sex. In the wild, lions mate for life—for the most part. Females stick with one mate but males have several main squeezes and stay with their harem for life. (Kind of like Mormons.) But for lions in the bush, having more than one ladylion is more a matter of survival and a guarantee to keep the pride plentiful and strong, spreading their seed around to keep numbers up. It has less to do with lust and more to do with Darwinism—survival of the fittest and all that.

On the whole, Leos are filled with love and affection, even if they do tend to come on very strong. They can get impatient when their needs aren't filled but their frankness and directness in bed is a breath of fresh air. The mirror opposite of Moon Children, who expect you to guess what they crave. Another reason they're not a good match for each other between the sheets.

The Leo Diet

To envision the perfect Leo diet, you have to think of a lion on the African savannah munching away on gazelle, zebra and anything else they can sink their chops into. The human Leo needs meat, meat and more meat—did I say meat?—and cooked as rare as you can manage without it walking off the plate.

Ray contends that any other Sun Sign that kept the Leo diet would be constipated forever. A bit TMI, however extremely true. Leo doesn't digest greens and fiber well. Their systems do much better with red meat. High blood pressure and high cholesterol don't usually plague them because they tend to be sinewy as hell and pure muscle. Leos need mountains of juicy redness to fuel their intense lifestyle. However, they can tolerate a bit of whole grains on the side—again, think savannah grasses—to keep them regular.

Game meats like boar, elk and venison are also pleasing to those born under this Sun Sign, as well as dark, meaty-tasting fowl like duck. Deep, complex pork roasts like pernil are other favorites among Leo.

These astrological lions are also attracted to rich, ballsy flavors of curries and spices like cumin and cilantro that permeate Latin American cuisine. Not hot and spicy but more savory. They are also drawn to intense, strong-tasting and smelling selections like caviar and smoked fish.

Leos are typically blessed with robust constitutions. In additions to meats and other simple proteins, they need to introduce a bit of grains and greens into their diet—even though these are not what they naturally crave. All types of nuts, especially walnuts and almonds are important for their diets, as well as grains like whole wheat and rye. "Dark" root vegetables like beets and carrots are also beneficial.

But because the heart is Leo's ruling Bodypart, their usually hardy pumpers are also susceptible to disease. Special care must be taken to maintain a heart-healthy diet, Ray contends. Extra helpings of whole grains, green, leafy veggies and lean proteins are recommended.

An overdose of dairy products isn't recommended, especially those high in fat, because Leo doesn't process them well. But sweet indulgences like a fine dark chocolate can be a tasty treat, in addition to being heart-friendly.

Keeping to their naturally-inclined, protein-heavy diet generally doesn't cause problems but Leos should have regular check-ups to be sure their cholesterol levels don't spike. Because of all the red meat their bodies require and crave, they need to consume more of the less fatty cuts like round roasts and sirloin. When available, healthier alternatives like grass-fed beef should be selected. It's more expensive but the more healthful alternative for hardcore carnivores like Leo.

Fire signs like Leo are full of energy (fire) and need warm, fleshy dishes to thrive. They should eat plenty of foods rich in magnesium—in addition to the foods mentioned above, they should try figs, rice, egg yolks, apples and peaches—and plentiful in iron—like raisins, spinach, grapes and broccoli—in addition to their beloved meaty meats.

Virgo
August 24 – September 23

Element: Earth

Heavenly Body: Mercury

Symbol: The Virgin

Stone: Sapphire

Lifequest: To be noble and righteous in all

Vibe: Kind and nurturing

Dirty Little Secret: I want be loved by you—and by everyone.

Bodypart: The nervous system and bowels

Fuelfoods: Pure, healthy foods, heavy on the salads and organics

Sign Song: "A Cockeyed Optimist"

Movie: *The 40 Year Old Virgin*—Virgos should find this charmingly silly ditty about a lovably nerdy fellow who is his own worst enemy both telling and sweet.

All About Virgo

Virgo is one of those poor Sun Signs that always gets bad-mouthed. Many astrologers paint the Virgin as being picky, narrow-minded and difficult, but not me. Seriously, some of my best friends are Virgos. I know (and love) them as being fastidious, determined, detail-oriented and devoted. A Virgo will do almost anything for anyone, even a stranger. And if you're a friend, there's no end to their generosity—of the spirit as well as of the pocketbook.

The problem is that Virgos are so kind, giving and gullible that it's very easy to take advantage of them. And unfortunately, some do. But instead of seeing these sparkling Virgo qualities as signs of weakness, I view them as remarkable strengths. So, their big hearts don't indicate a problem with Virgos but with the rest of the universe. If the world was more plentiful with these Virgins, there would be no war, no conflict of any sort. My apologies if this sounds sappy but it's true.

When Virgo shines, it's with a warm internal light. And because Virgo is an Earth Sign, it's a different sort of glow than Fire Signs possess. Virgo's brilliance shimmers quietly from within and it's wonderfully contagious, touching everything in its path with its amazingly positive vibe. Take it from me, you're a much better person having a Virgo in your life.

Because Mercury is their ruling planet, Virgos are busy "do-ers." Like the gods' famed messenger symbolized by the smallest planet, Virgo is committed to zipping from one thing to the next, fixing, patching, mending and making things better for everyone else.

When the Virgin is content and sure of itself, it's a blessing to know them. But when they are insecure and self-depreciating, it's indeed a sad sight to see. A well-adjusted Virgo comfortable in their own skin is an absolute pleasure to meet. When they have their act together, Virgos are among the most successful, organized and imaginative peeps in the entire Zodiac.

Take a look at a handful of "famous" Virgos—Leonard Bernstein, Sean Connery, Elvis Costello, Mother Teresa, Jack Black, Ingrid Bergman, John Coltrane, Rocky Marciano, Roald Dahl, Lily Tomlin, Moby, Warren Buffett, Gloria Estefan, John McCain, Charlie Sheen, Pink, Ivan the Terrible, Sophia Loren, Tim Burton, Agatha Christie, O. Henry, Jose Feliciano and Joan Jett—and you'll find a diverse, talented, sometimes tortured group. A number of notable Virgos have met untimely endings, including Cass Elliot and Michael Jackson, a sad illustration of the fate of talented Virgos who aren't in tune with their magic.

Virgins are "givers" rather than "takers." In everyday life, you'll find a disproportionate number of Virgos who dedicate their lives to the service of others. Selfless folks like social workers, judges, doctors and school teachers to healers like massage therapists and acupuncturists. Not only are they extremely good at their chosen careers but they enjoy their callings immensely. Virgos tend to immerse themselves wholeheartedly into what they believe in, be it their work or their relationships.

One of Virgo's best—and worst—qualities is their optimism. No matter how many times they get stomped by life or hurt in relationships, they still have faith in others and are never touched by cynicism. Their sunny attitude epitomizes Anne Frank's quote: "Despite everything, I believe that people are really good at heart." (Dear Annie, by the way, was Gemini but with a moon in Virgo.)

And by worst quality, I mean that Virgo's exceedingly good nature is all too often exploited by others. Unfortunately, they are frequently mistreated and are commonly victims of swindle schemes, overworked and taken advantage of, especially in relationships. That's why they are complimented by relationships with strong Sun Signs like Taurus, Pisces and Capricorn.

Don't get me wrong, it's not that Virgo is a weak sign, quite the opposite, it's just that people mistake their goodness for a flaw, then stomp all over it. That's why they need a bull-like Taurus to stand up for them.

Understandably, Virgos are usually very sensitive. They also tend to be shy, content to let others take the spotlight, even though they're often the "brains" behind an operation. However, just knowing that they helped accomplish greatness is rewarding enough for Virg. They're also often the man or woman behind the man or woman, perfectly happy giving their partner the tools they need to blossom.

And speaking of blossoms, I like to think of this Sun Sign as being a rare and delicate rose which needs a gentle hand and tender care in order to thrive. It's a perfect analogy of the Virgo inner beauty and profound goodness.

These Virgins of the Zodiac are also creative geniuses. They're unusually gifted musically (and when they are, they generally play several instruments and play them like virtuosos). Virgos can also be talented writers. But because they're so cerebral, it can take them a long time to create a piece of music or writing. In order to do so, everything has to be in order—and a specific order at that—so they can create, and nothing can make them deviate from that order. One Virgo pal of ours is a skilled writer but forces herself to go through a number of drafts, whether or not Draft 1 is perfect. Because of this, Dottie can't work fast and thus loses out on opportunities because she compels herself to do rewrites that aren't always necessary.

But when life hands you lemons and you need someone in your corner, there's no better "someone" than a Virgo. They will give you their prized lemonade recipe and patiently guide you through each step until you can do it on your own. They're level-headed advice-givers and the most loyal of friends.

Because Virgos are ultra-sensitive themselves, I think they truly and deeply understand human frailties better than almost anyone else. Not only does Virgo empathize but they honestly, profoundly care. Having a Virgo as a friend or lifepartner can be an unbelievably rewarding experience.

Virgo Between the Sheets

Poor Virgo! They've also gotten a bad rap as being prudish toward sex. But just like their general horoscope prognosis, this isn't exactly the case. Virgo has a very healthy attitude toward sex—and this might be where the misconception lies.

The Virgin approaches acts erotic the way they do everything else: pragmatically. To Virgo, sex is simply a necessary part of life in order to keep the body beautiful running smoothly. It's therapeutic, much like any other form of exercise plus it's a great tension releaser.

Not very sexy? No, but that's the way it is with Virgo—what you see is what you get. I wouldn't go so far as to call sex a necessary evil but to the practical Virgo, it is what it is. Most of these Virgins don't frequently get what you call randy or horny, they might just look at the calendar and think, "Hey, it's been a while...Time to flush out the pipes. Let's do it." So much for pillowtalk.

A host of Virgos get turned on by what might be referred to as Plain Jims and Janes—the slightly nerdy bespectacled fellow in the next cubicle... "Lovely Rita, Meter Maid." You get the idea, someone who's simple, uncomplicated, nice. A Virgoian buddy of mine had a serious case of the hots for the local TV weathergirl. To me, she was a bit on the milquetoast side and a wee bit homey, but Thomas swore "she could get nasty" just by watching the way she wielded a pointer. He pined for her endlessly and ended up marrying a gal who looked a lot like her.

Many Virgos actually prefer a basic, no-frills partner. To them, it's just easier that way. Less maintenance, more practical.

In fact, some Virgs are like this themselves—not much to look at, but just below the surface they have a depth and intensity that is jaw-dropping. And oh-so-rewarding for those willing to peel away the succulent layers of the artichoke to get to the tasty heart.

Virgos are extremely attentive and respectful lovers. Their partner definitely comes first. The Virgin's supreme kindness carries over into the bedroom by doing thoughtful, little things for their mates. It's not unusual to find a shiny trinket or a succulent chocolate on your pillow when you share the Virgin's bed. Just the knowledge that they're appreciated by a partner is thanks enough for them.

The Virgin's nurturing tendencies also mean that they like fixing things, especially in bed. Male and female V's love to take an inexperienced partner under their wings and show them the ropes, so to speak. But in the kindest, most compassionate way.

Despite their reputations as neat freaks, Virgos aren't above getting their hands dirty in the boudoir. Sticky fingers and other bodyparts don't put them off, just so long as there's somewhere to clean up afterwards. While they might be a bit self-conscious about their own shortcomings and imperfections, they'll heartily embrace and accept yours. In fact, they won't see them as shortcomings at all.

Since most Virgos are naturally submissive, they get super aroused by the notion that they're a sexual slave who is "forced" to do all sorts of "revolting" things. For the Virgin, who spends so much time living in their own head, being told what to do gives them a breather. They have no trouble letting somebody else do the driving—or the spanking.

Ditto for being a voyeur. Says Dr. Vivian, the very act of watching also frees the watcher from responsibility. They're looking rather than doing. They're not initiating. They're being swept along with the current instead of being compelled into making decisions. So the voyeur isn't exactly helpless but more closely, an "innocent" bystander. Many people find this truly liberating—Virgos, in particular.

So you see, these Virgins aren't quite the prudish lovers they're made out to be. More specifically, they're prone to being modest and a bit shy between the sheets. However, if you help Virgos feel comfortable and safe, you'll be rewarded with an attentive, curious partner who just needs a little bidding to break out of their shell. In other words, someone "who can get wild."

True to their Sun Sign's hype, Virgo can be very, very picky, especially when choosing a bedmate. Most would rather go without sex or without a steady partner rather than just settle for a meaningless one-nighter. So, when you get selected by a Virgo, consider it a great compliment.

The Virgo Diet

Earthy Virgo is a purist when it comes to food. They are the most likely astrological sign to be health nuts and buy organic. In fact, the word "organic" makes their hearts skip a beat. I'll go so far as to wager that there are more vegetarians and vegans among Virgos than any other Sun Sign.

Virgins can wax philosophical about all of the varieties of brown rice in their local grocer. They can tell you in great detail about the history of spelt and how whole wheat berries differ from the ever-superior farro. For Virgo, raw rules...and I'm not talking about meat. If they do partake in the cooked flesh, it's usually well done, not a speck of blood on the plate.

Ray says that Virgos, whose ruling Bodypart is the bowels (and intestines), along with the nervous system, are usually able to tolerate and easily digest large amounts of plant matter. Yep, they're a lot like cows, with one highly-evolved gizzard doing the work of the bovine's four convenient stomach sections. The Virgo belly and bowels can handle a whole lot of greens and then some.

In particular, Virgos need leafy green veggies like spinach and kale, whole wheat and whole grain breads, oats, almonds, cheeses, oranges, bananas, lemons, melons, apples, pear and papaya in order to keep their systems in fine working order. A dream meal for a Virgo of a ginormous salad of mixed greens would have a meat loving Leo or Aries asking, "Yeah, but seriously...what's for dinner."

Virgos are often accused of having a "nervous stomach," but this is only when they tax their systems with an abundance of processed foods. If a Virgo doesn't stick to the raw rule, they are prone to weight-gain. Although they love chocolate, it doesn't love them back, and can result in skin eruptions and upset tummies. Heavy foods wreak havoc on their delicate digestive systems, which function best with "earthy" foods in their pure form...directly from the garden.

Because they're prone to obsessive tendencies, Virgo's compulsion with natural foods can carry over into other areas, more specifically health, exercise and hygiene. You know the type—the world will fall off its axis if they don't do 300 sit-ups a day or if they miss their spin class. They're the ones wearing the protective facemask when they visit New York City—"All of that nasty pollution, you know." They were voted "Most Likely to Have Obsessive Compulsive Disorder" in junior high. V's have no problem walking out of a restaurant because they don't like the looks of the chef.

But given lots of TLC, pep talks and a long leash, Virgos can learn how to keep their OCD reigned in, relax and enjoy life. I promise.

Libra

September 24 – October 23

Element: Air

Heavenly Body: Venus

Symbol: The Scales

Stone: Opal

Lifequest: To achieve balance

Vibe: Wavering

Dirty Little Secret: I need consistency and a firm hand to guide me.

Bodypart: The lower back and buttocks

Fuelfoods: Has a wicked sweet tooth—will choose chocolate over a meal

Sign Song: "Venus"

Movie: *Midnight in the Garden of Good and Evil*—A classic Libra film brimming with conflict and people who look beneficent but are really bad to the bone.

All About Libra

Okay, I admit, because I am a Libra, this was the hardest astrological profile for me to write. It always is. Vivian and Ray really had to reel me on this one. But how can I not expound upon the fact that Libra is the most wonderful sign of the Zodiac? But seriously, I have tried to stand back and remain objective, offering a combination of personal insight and professional expertise concerning this Sun Sign.

On the surface, Libra appears to be a very even, steady, stable member of the Zodiac family. I mean, just look at those solid, sturdy scales. But in reality, the life of a Libra is a constant struggle to achieve—and then maintain—balance. It's a balancing act pure and simple.

Librans traditionally take on more than they can handle—and they like to think they can handle just about anything. They have a difficult time saying no (to anyone or anything), so more often than not, their plate isn't so much as full as it is overflowing. What many Librans (myself included) don't understand is that refusing these numerous, and sometimes unreasonable, requests is the way they can achieve their much-sought-after equilibrium.

A Libra would rather exasperate themselves than fail someone. They'd rather pull an all-nighter to make an impossible deadline or deny themselves a night on the town to babysit for a friend in need. If you want a task done, ask a busy Libra—not only will it get done but it will get done ahead of time.

In many ways, Libra is hung up on the Disney fantasy—that "some day my prince (or princess) will come" and then everything will magically be perfect. This daydream is usually fueled early on, in childhood or adolescence, and it makes an indelible mark on their lives. In most cases, this ruins the Scales by skewing their sense of "real" romance. Which definitely ain't made to order by Disney!

So, the "real world" can be a rude awakening for this dreamy Sun Sign. For me personally, growing up in a loving household, I felt that I was beautiful and special—until I realized that in the outside world, I was just like everyone else. Couple this harsh realization with typical teenage broken hearts, an awkward, gawky stage and the usual disappointments. I had quite a tough adjustment period and a notoriously stinky adolescence until I blossomed in my early 20s.

As a Venus-ruled sign, Libra puts love first and foremost, so lost love really packs a wallop for them. Ultra-sensitive Libras have a tougher time recovering from breakups and disappointments than many of their thicker-skinned Zodiac companions, even Taurus, who is also guided by Venus.

Never forget that Libra lives are a quest for balance. This realization will help you understand them (and your Libra self) better. To the rest of the planet, they might seem perfectly in tune with themselves and in control, but it's usually just a brilliant disguise they've mastered throughout the years. Often, their sunny attitude in the face of stormy weather is just a perfectly-played masquerade.

In order to function at their best, Libras need consistency and have no problem being guided or led. In fact, they seek it out. Although Librans can be "idea people" they truly shine when given an idea they can run with. This is one reason they make the best employees—they're hard-working, determined, inventive and consistently blow their bosses out of the water with their knack for nailing whatever assignment or chore they're given.

We Librans have the uncanny ability to tune out and zone in on our inner rhythms, blocking out the rest of the world. It's been said that this Sun Sign can live in their heads, almost to a fault because in doing this, they face the danger of denying their true destinies, which exist beyond their heads.

Libras are literally chameleons—they can morph into anything they need to be. The Scales can "play" at being a business person or a teacher so convincingly that they begin to believe it themselves, even if it's not in their nature. For Librans, not only does this brand of play-acting give them a chance to stretch their creative muscles but it also gives them a breather from their inner demons. A mini-vacation from themselves, if you will.

All of the Goddess of Love's seductive wiles make Libra disarmingly charming. A Libran can pretty much get whatever they want when they set their minds to it. Their charisma can win them jobs, get them into exclusive clubs, woo influential friends... There's no limit to what a Libran wink and a smile can accomplish! But luckily, this magnetic Sun Sign is also highly moral and generally uses their powers for good, not for evil.

Some noteworthy Librans are Johns Entwistle and Lennon (who were both born on my birthday), Julie Andrews, Chuck Berry, Kim Kardashian, Gandhi, Lillian Gish, Lenny Bruce, Martina Navratilova, Dizzy Gillespie, Truman Capote, Jimmy Carter, Serena Williams, Oscar Wilde, Eminem, Johnny Carson, Eleanor Roosevelt, Caravaggio, Nietzsche, Donna Karan, Snoop Dogg, Anne Rice, Will Smith, Lee Iacocca, Mickey Mantle, ee cummings, Catherine Zeta-Jones, Michael Douglas, Barbara Walters, et al.

A fun Libra fact: an inordinately large number of Libras were born on September 25, notably the last three on the above list. Why, you might ask? It's exactly nine months to the day after Christmas. Talk about the amorous Christmas gift that doesn't quit!

Although Libras place so much emphasis on relationships, it's sad to say that many Libras stink at choosing an appropriate partner—in business and in bed. A number of Libras would fare much better if they forged ahead alone. But alas, "alone" isn't part of their vocabulary.

For lucky Librans (like me!) who are blessed to find their soul mate (in my case, after a few false starts and one icky marriage), their life can indeed be charmed. You're apt to find Libras in creative careers which have chosen them rather than the other way around—writers, musicians, designers or artists, for example. Most Librans know what they want to be early on in life because they've had a calling of sorts.

Libras can also be entrepreneurs. Perfect example: Anita Roddick, founder of The Body Shop. Look for them as proprietors of a funky restaurant, owners of an offbeat business or even astrologers, like *moi*. These free spirits don't usually thrive in traditional business settings or in highly-structured environments or organizations, but if they are found in an office, it has to be on their own terms. They're the CEO who wears zany ties or brightly-colored socks beneath their Armani suits.

The desire to do anything to avoid a conflict can lead Libras into sticky situations, which is why they tend to say "yes" when they mean "no." They hate to disappoint, to let anyone down. They also hate the idea that someone might not like them, so they will do everything within their power to make themselves likeable.

Many consider Libras to be very attractive—or at least that's the way they're perceived. They're so vivacious that they appear to be things of beauty, even if they aren't what you'd call classically beautiful. Again, Libra's strong roots in Venus is to blame. It's also responsible for their deep appreciation of the arts.

Decision-making is an issue for Libras. They are terrible wafflers because they can see both sides of every situation, usually more. Libran indecisiveness can be extremely annoying to other Zodiac-ers.

The perfect mate for Libra is Aries. Their cut-and-dry nature can snap a wavering Libra into shape, so they balance out each other perfectly. Also good pairings for Librans are Gemini and Aquarius. But the right mate can perfectly compliment Libra's quest for stability and make them feel secure. Then all of their beautiful opaline facets will shine at their brightest.

Libra Between the Sheets

With Libra, their pleasure is your pleasure. There goes that quest for balance again! It even carries over into bed for these children of Venus. Librans seek perfection in their relationships and are often disappointed...but then the right one comes along. When a Libra is happy in love, then all is well with their world because love is clearly the center of their universe.

This sign is extremely amorous and erotic—there goes Venus again. They are quietly seductive in and out of the bedroom. Just one look from a Libra is usually enough to send even the most stony-hearted Scorpio into a tailspin. They are givers, which is also good news for their mates. But Libras aren't above balancing out the genital generosity with a little something-something for themselves too.

With a Libra lover, you will also have a tremendously creative sex partner. They like to catch you off guard, so expect the unexpected. Afternoon delights are a favorite of theirs. So is waking up their beau in the middle of the night with an oral surprise.

Yes, they are very orally oriented, so Libras don't usually have a problem telling you exactly what they want—and need in bed. These scales weigh either one way or the other—either they're hopeless romantics or nymphomaniacs. Your job...find out which one you're bedding!

Libras can also be offbeat lovers and aren't adverse to role-playing games, as long as they are balanced and don't go overboard. A little hair-pulling, a bit of spanking, a touch of dirtytalk, but nothing too over the top. Variety is the spice of their lustfires, but not too much variety, you understand. They like it slightly rough but fair—cross that line and get too nasty and they can fold up like a Venus flytrap.

Libra's dominant Bodyparts are their lower back and buttocks. Females tend to have especially elegant lumbar regions and curvy behinds. Males typically have nicely muscled, well-shaped, strapping backs. Yes, Libra ladies usually have prominent, curvaceous nether cheeks that beg for a little swat now and again.

Want an insider's tip? Give your Libra a backrub down where the base of their spine meets their bottom. Not only will they melt in your hands but they'll be yours forever.

But not if the sheets are mussed! Libras can also be almost as fussy as their Virgo Zodiac neighbors! They like to flop into a nicely-made bed and have been known not to be able to orgasm if the linens aren't perfectly straight beneath their bodies. If the mood and atmosphere isn't just right, it could be a deal-breaker. But if a Libra's happy then everyone's happy. Especially between the sheets!

The Libra Diet

Libra's love of sweets is legendary. More than any other Sun Sign, they run the risk of being diabetic and/or overweight. Ray contends that by overweight, he doesn't mean morbidly obese, but carrying a few extra pounds around the middle or the bottom (where it tends to collect for those in this Zodiac group). Libras are much too vain to go overboard in this area! Being 10 or 20 pounds overweight, springs them into dieting action. They'll lose a few kilos, then might even balloon back up again if their indulgence goes unchecked. So, Libras take heed how you feed!

Librans have a serious sweet tooth that will not be ignored. I've made peace with mine by allowing myself one small, fine, delicious piece of chocolate each night. Just one! I look forward to it all day, savor it, then am satiated...until the next day. I am such a chocoholic that even my vitamins are chocolate flavored.

Because of this tendency to overindulge at the dessert bar of life, Libra must take special care to eat healthily, Ray warns. Although it doesn't come naturally, Librans must force themselves to eat a balanced diet (there's that word again) filled with fruits and vegetables, whole grains and lean protein.

A weird quirk I've noticed about Libras: they eat evenly. Meaning, if they have a plate of meat, potatoes and veg, they will steadily sample a forkful from each, until there's just one mouthful of their favorite item left. No gorging on the steak first, then finishing all of the mashed potatoes and saving that pile of spinach for last. Nope, Libras will take a bite of steak, then a taste of spuds, then a forkful of greens before going back to the meat. I thought everybody ate like that until another friend pointed out that only I ate like that. Well, me and *all* my Libra buddies.

Because it's one of their ruling Bodyparts, Librans tend to carry around all of their tension in their lower spines. So when they're feeling especially stressed, it's not uncommon for their backs to go out just above the coccyx. It's important for Libras to stretch, so yoga is a great release for them. Their kidneys, located in the lower back region, are also trouble-spots, and they are prone to infections, kidney pain and urinary ailments. In addition to including kidney healthy foods—like cranberries—in their diets, hydration is also key for them.

Other good foods for Libra are strawberries, asparagus, spinach, beets, and whole grains like brown rice and oatmeal. High-protein diets provide the perfect fuel for this high-energy Air sign, but be sure to limit the fat, sugar and acidic foods. Pork and beef should be shied away from, opting instead for broiled fish, seafood and poultry.

In keeping with their "even eating syndrome," dishes that go perfectly with Libra sensibilities are balanced one pot meals like stews (equal parts meat and veg) and thick, hearty soups (which usually contain a little bit of everything).

Scorpio
October 24 – November 22

Element: Water

Heavenly Body: Pluto

Symbol: The Scorpion

Stone: Topaz

Lifequest: To come out on top against all odds

Vibe: Tough and durable

Dirty Little Secret: I need to win—always, at any cost.

Bodyparts: The genitals

Fuelfoods: Intense foods with strong tastes including smoked fish and stinky cheeses

Sign Song: "I Will Survive"

Movie: *Defiance*—The heroic story of survival and triumph against all odds in the forests of WWII Russia is a Scorpio must-see.

All About Scorpio

Like Virgo, Scorpio is another Sun Sign that consistently gets a bad rap. But with the Virgin, it's for being "too good." For Scorpio, it's (quite unfairly) for being "too bad." To the Scorpion's defense, I will say that extreme strength is all too often seen as a negative. I aim to set that record straight here.

Scorpio lays claim to being the most powerful sign of the Zodiac and few would dispute this fact. They are tough as iron, as determined as that tortoise in Aesop's fable as and have a poisonous bite which is best manifested in their sharp tongue. But on the upside, to be loved by a Scorpio is to be loved fiercely and unrelentlessly. Which could also be a downside, depending on your POV. There's a fine line between love and captivity. (Unless you happen to be into that!)

My father was a Scorpio, and a very typical one. He was a force to be reckoned with and heavens help you if you disagreed with or crossed him. There is nothing quite so stormy or so scary as the wrath of a Scorpio. Even just a wicked glance from them can wilt a lesser man or woman.

As children, Scorpios are usually mature well beyond their years, quiet and contemplative. Whether this is because of who they are or just a matter of circumstance is debatable. In my dad's case, he lived in a household with an alcoholic parent, so he was used to playing silently and acting like a grown-up, even when he was five. But I think he would have been an introspective little fellow, no matter what. That's the Scorpion in him. They are indeed old souls, even as toddlers, and so wise that it can be disarming in the young.

Adult Scorpios think they have all the answers—and usually do!—for the world's problems, and most importantly, for you. Try to imagine what it's like growing up with a Scorpio parent. My dad and I were constantly butting heads, and because he was the dominant Sun Sign—and the head of household—he usually won out. But to his credit, Dad was a fantastic provider, a staunch protector and fiercely proud of my accomplishments. Textbook Scorpio traits.

Scorpio are adept at figuring out what's best for others, but sadly, those born under this Sun Sign often have a tough time deciphering what's best for themselves and knowing the key ingredients to their own happiness.

The Scorpion's life is marked by fate, which not only guides them but rules them. Scorpios are intense by nature and therefore tend to have dramatic personal relationships. Suitable mates for Scorpio include those born under the sign of Virgo and Pisces, which have a knack for diluting Scorpio's volatile nature. But my gentle Gemini mom was also a pro at keeping my explosive dad at bay.

Passion, desire and power are one in the same for Scorpios. Their most potent challenge in life is deciphering which is more important—the love of power or the power of love. It's a debacle that will haunt them all of their lives.

Living or working with the Scorpion is an emotional roller coaster ride because of Scorpio's constant challenge of coming to grips with their own deep, intense feelings—about just about everything. People often feel as though they're walking on eggshells around them...which they are. Scorpios are a wildly unique astrological sign, so everything they do is unlike anyone else. The way they answer the phone, butter their toast, the way they kiss or tell a joke, all 100% distinctive.

Family members and mates of the Scorpion often tell me that although they've spent years with their Scorpio loved one, they never truly feel as though they know them. Much about that creature is a mystery—symbolized by their soft, vulnerable body hidden beneath a hard, protective shell. As additional layers of protection, they even have a set of knife-like claws and a venomous stinger to keep predators at bay. Who can dare to even attempt to hug a creature like that?

The best way to deal with a Scorpio is by sheer instinct, almost telepathically, by intuition. Their shell is their mask. Similar to Libra, they often say "no" when they mean "yes" and vice versa. But for Scorpio, it isn't because they hate to let people down but it's because they absolutely love playing the devil's advocate; it fuels them.

Be forewarned, you'll never win an argument with a Scorpio, so don't even try. Just agree to disagree—if they let you.

Scorpios are highly competitive and because of this drive to succeed, they usually come out victorious. One thing that can hold them back, however, is their badass attitudes. They can easily get caught up in the positive or negative of a situation which either propels them forward or destroys them.

In other words, The Scorpion can be their own worst enemy if they're steeped in negativity. Similarly, the optimistic Scorpio can successfully sail through a sea of adversity by the power of their positive attitude alone.

Noteworthy Scorpios are Pablo Picasso, Hillary Clinton, Sylvia Plath, Bill Gates, Winona Ryder, Marie Antoinette, Ike Turner, Marie Curie, Kevin Kline, Katy Perry, P Diddy, Joni Mitchell, Kurt Vonnegut, Tracy Morgan, Auguste Rodin, Julia Roberts, Neil Young, Whoppi Goldberg, Ryan Gosling, RuPaul, Martin Scorsese, Ken Griffey, Jr., Martin Luther, Voltaire, Nelly, Scarlett Johansson and Robert Kennedy. Talk about strong!

Much like Leo, this Zodialogical creature operates on three distinct planes that can very likely operate out of sequence. Scorpios are so unpredictable and volatile that they can go through various stages of these three levels in one lifetime:

- **Phoenix Rising** – These highly-evolved Scorpios are loners and super-charged with power. Astute even as youngsters, they're born leaders and super-inspiring;

- **Eagle** – Soaring, industrious and thriving, this incarnation transcends hardship and skillfully morphs negatives into positives; and

- **Scorpion** – The most raw evolvement, they are drawn to "the Dark Side" (think Darth Vader) and using their powers for evil.

Everything is black or white for a Scorpio, good or bad, desirable or ho-hum. That's why they make such great police officers, judges and attorneys. Cut and dry, yes, but Scorpios also cut to the chase, not like the forever indecisive Libra. Scorpions love to pull things apart then piece them back together again— and when they do, they're often in better shape than they were to start with. Mechanics, carpenters, handymen (and women) are some careers they gravitate toward—and excel at.

Since Scorpio is ruled by Pluto (the recently-demoted planet and god of the underworld), it possesses an intense energy that can easily turn dark. Scorpions are known to have bad tempers and can go from carefree to cranky in a matter of seconds. This Water Sign's mood can change as quickly as the sea. But if you're fortunate enough to be on the upside of their beneficence, you'll know no better companion or mate.

Scorpio Between the Sheets

In the bedroom, Scorpio's erotic battle can be described as the sexual vs. the sensual. Simply put, they are the horndogs of the Zodiac! The Scorpion's magnetic personality and strong sense of self makes them forces to be reckoned between the sheets. Since Scorpions are so complex sexually they are deep, intense and multi-faceted lovers.

Here's the scoop—Scorpios get off on power. They love, love, love role-playing games where they're in charge (no surprise here) and get to wield their might over poor unsuspecting victims. The Scorpion enjoys making a partner cower, grovel, even sob, then try to win back their approval. Both men and women born under this Sun Sign enjoy heavy-duty power-play and have no trouble enacting Master/Mistress and slave fantasies, because for them, these scenarios don't stray far from the truth.

Scorpios are also taboo-breakers. They are game for anything if there's the promise of an orgasm at the end of the tunnel. Scorpio embrace their fetishes (as everyone should, reminds Dr. Vivian) and often have more than one offbeat fantasy that they're perfectly willing to share with deserving partners who'd also like to play.

Unfortunately, Scorpios are the least likely Zodiac sign to be monogamous. This isn't because they're unable but because most often, they don't have the desire. However, if the Scorpion has a faithful streak, then they can be extremely dedicated and true. But it's all up to Scorpio what kind of partner they choose to be. For this reason, open relationships are often good options for this Sun Sign.

Physically, those born under the Scorpio moon tends to have very voluptuous bodies—men as well as women. I've always believed that this is an outward manifestation of their inward—and all encompassing—sexual life.

Did I mention that this Sun Sign is highly erotic? Scorpio women are prone to full-body multiple orgasms which are so intense they can frighten away faint-hearted lovers. Scorpio men tend to have extremely copious emissions—i.e. they come in buckets! Partners will have no trouble admitting that Scorpio climaxes are so strong they feel as though they're spasming along with their Scorpion lovers.

Because their ruling Bodypart are the genitals, Scorpios are prone to having issues "down there"—cystitis, skin eruptions, serious urinary tract infections and even venereal diseases. Scorpions should take special care to practice safe sex, use condoms and use discretion in partners. Dr. Vivian adds that all Sun Signs should adhere to this, but Scorpio even moreso.

Although they love "the act" intensely, Scorpions have been known to abstain from sex just to prove a point—or punish—a partner. They get off by holding back almost as much as they do letting go. Sex is primarily a power play for Scorpio and you know how they feel about power!

Aggressive in bed, many Scorpios prefer sexual encounters anyplace but—in stairwells, cars, movie theatres, the riskier the better. Prone to excesses, Scorpios are more likely to be considered sex addicts than any other Sun Sign.

Not only are these Scorpions provocative but they're also incredibly private. Your sexual secret is safe with a Scorpio and rarely do they *schtupp* and tell.

The Scorpio Diet

A good match for their intense personalities, most Scorpios enjoy indulging in extremely intense foods. Toe-curling goat cheese (sorry Capricorn!), bring it on. The more fetid the feta, the better. Smoked mackerel, liverwurst, horseradish, stinky sushi (like uni), raw garlic...all yummy foods to Scorpions.

However, Scorpio prefers whatever's on their plate to be as no-nonsense and ballsy as they are. Their palate is rich and intense. You can't go wrong with putting aromatic olive oils, vinegar-soaked olives, capers, sardines and smoked oysters on a Scorpio's table.

To balance the acidity brought on by indulging in many of these foods, Scorpios need a diet that includes a larger number of calcium-rich foods than most other Sun Signs require. It's important to balance their intense systems with cooling, calming choices like milk, cheese, yogurt and cottage cheese, tells Ray.

Other recommended (and often neglected) food selections for Scorpios are fish, seafood, green salads, beets, lentils, nuts (especially almonds and walnuts), citrus fruits, berries, apples, bananas and pineapples.

Unfortunately, Scorpio's excessive personality gives them a natural proclivity toward abuses. No other Sun Sign is more predisposed to being binge eaters (and purgers), alcoholics, substance abusers, or to having eating disorders. Hard liquor in particular is problematic and its effects wreak havoc on sensitive Scorpio skin. Can you say "gin blossom nose?"

Scorpios should avoid large meals. A much better option would be several smaller meals throughout the day to fuel the

Scorpio fires. And bottled or filtered water is preferable over tap water. It's easier on their digestive systems.

Sagittarius
November 23 – December 21

Element: Fire

Heavenly Body: Jupiter

Symbol: The Archer/The Centaur

Stone: Turquoise

Lifequest: Pursuit of "the good life"

Vibe: Explosive with predictable blowups

Dirty Little Secret: I want everyone to know my name.

Bodyparts: The hips region (including the thighs, pelvis and femur)

Fuelfoods: Fragrant, yet no-nonsense foods that include a little bit of everything—think *bouillabaisse*, *cioppino* and Moroccan stews.

Sign Song: "Don't Fence Me In"

Movie: *Beauty and the Beast*—Yeah, it's a cartoon but nothing captures this Sun Sign's human/animal conflict so perfectly or charmingly.

All About Sagittarius

No Sun Sign has a *joie de vivre* quite like Sagittarius. Their natural high, adventurous heart and unrestrained joy is infectious. Although they can be one of the most buoyant, hopeful members of the Zodiac, unfortunately, they can also be among the most bleak and dismal. Nobody is as downright joyful as a Sag but no one is as downhearted when things don't quite go their way. It was a tossup between their Sign Song being "Don't Fence Me In" and "Manic Depressive," but I opted for the more positive option.

Dr. V contends that some born under the glow of Jupiter have dangerously unhealthy mood swings, so much so that they can have suicidal thoughts. (If this rings true for you or anyone you know, we urge you to seek professional help. There are many trained therapists, like Vivian, who will guide you to safer ground.) But many more Sagittarians learn how to control their soaring highs and down-in-the-basement lows by using their strong minds and powerful wills.

Think of the arrow this Sun Sign's Archer shoots. It can pierce the heavens one second then come crashing down into the dirt the next. Even though it can be a struggle for Sagittarius to function on an even kilter, it is extremely possible for them to do so with hard work and self control.

However, the Sagittarian optimism is truly something to behold. They set their sights on their heart's desire—be it the perfect job, an alluring mate, their dream home, the trip of a lifetime—and most often, by hook or by crook, they get it. Sags live by the belief that anything is possible and this positive outlook carries them through—most of the time. They are victorious—most of the time. But when they're not, it takes a

115

great deal of time and effort to lure them out of their frighteningly dark doldrums.

Perhaps because Sagittarius is symbolized by a creature that is part human, part beast, they are difficult to fence in. Don't even try! The horse in them wants to roam the fields of life, explore, taste and experience. The human half generally does a good job of reeling in the beast and keeping their hooves grounded in reality. But when a Sagittarius is off balance, watch out. Both parts battle each other mercilessly and in the end, nobody wins.

Only the most fully-evolved Centaur learns to successfully integrate both their animal and human parts into one harmonious being. Others might spend a good deal of the time being at war with themselves if they don't acknowledge and embrace the wonders that make them them.

The Archer is arguably the most free and breezy sign of the Zodiac. They are forever on the move, testing out new religions, different cultures, obscure political viewpoints and unconventional schools of thought. This can be maddening to, say, a stiff and fussy Virgo, but Fire Signs like Aries or Leo can fight Sagittarius fire with fire, so to speak. Gemini might also be a good match, but only Gems with great patience and an especially sunny disposition.

True to their Sign Song, Sags don't like to be corralled and will buck like a raging bronco when forced to. It's quite unusual to find the Archer choosing careers that require a 9-5 office setting. More likely are they landscapers, real estate brokers, in sales, photojournalists, even teachers—anything that lets them work outside the box, or cubicle. Oh, they might have to spend a few hours in an office but the bulk of their job is done out in the field. Remember the college professor who moved class out onto the green when weather permitted? Most likely a Sagittarius.

Relationship-wise, be sure to keep your Sagittarius mate on a long leash or better yet, no leash at all. When thinking of these Centaurs in relationships, the old Richard Bach quote from *Jonathan Livingston Seagull* comes to mind—"If you love something, set it free; if it comes back, it's yours, if it doesn't it never was." That fits Sagittarius to a T.

Centaurs don't do well being forced into relationships or feeling tied down (literally or figuratively) against their will (so forget bondage of any kind—more about that in the next section). But if committing is their idea, or at least you make them think it's their idea, then they're all for it. Sagittarians need to keep their sense of self, their identities, at all costs.

Painfully honest, almost to a fault, Sagittarians will tell you with childlike candor that your dress does, in fact, make you look fat. But it's not with a Scorpio's meanness, for Sag it's with a blatant honesty and their wholehearted belief that the truth is the best medicine in all cases, even if it might sting like an arrow. Sags reason that the wound soon heals and then all you're left with is insight and you're much better for it. The truth shall set you free is their mantra, and Sagittarius is all about freedom.

Since Jupiter, this Sun Sign's ruling heavenly body, is the largest planet in our solar system, it has long been associated with abundance and excess. This explains the Centaur's generosity (almost to a fault) and their tendency to go overboard. Mythologically-speaking, Jupiter is also king of the gods, which explains Sag's strong sense of self and being masters of their own universe.

Those born under the ninth Sun Sign are Winston Churchill, Britney Spears, Andrew Carnegie, Nostradamus, Tina Turner, Mark Twain, Toulouse Lautrec, Jay-Z, Joe DiMaggio Jimi Hendrix, Bette Midler, Zachary Taylor, Richard Pryor, Lucy Liu, Carrie Nation, Bruce Lee, Billy Idol, Edith Piaf, Diego Rivera, Miley Cyrus, Walt Disney, Ty Cobb, Anna Nicole Smith, The Game, Woody Allen, Nelly Furtado, C.S. Lewis, Ozzy Osbourne, Shirley Chisholm, Milla Jovovich, Jamie Foxx, Marisa Tomei, Lucky Luciano, Mos Def, Brad Pitt and Frank Zappa. Lots of flamboyant individuals here.

It's not surprising that Sagittarians are often extremely athletic, especially when they allow the "horse" in them to fully develop. Because of their ruling body areas (hips, thighs and pelvis), they are usually excellent at long-distance activities like running, particularly endurance sports like marathons and triathlons.

Sags also love to laugh—and will keep you laughing until you cry. They usually have a wicked sense of humor and a knack for pointing out the absurd, which is a constant source of amusement for them. But on the other end of the spectrum, they can get hung up on depressing stats too, so the Centaur must make an effort not to go into that "dark room" because it can be difficult to find their way out.

Big-hearted, independent and spontaneous, relationships with the Archer of the Zodiac are generally rewarding if you keep it loose, open and unrestrained. Not the wild ride you'd have with an Aries, but full of surprises and complimented by the refreshingly Sagittarius sense of wonder. It might be a challenge, however, to learn how to deal with their exceptionally low lows, but worth the effort in the end.

Sagittarius Between the Sheets

Because they're basically kids at heart, Sagittarius like to have fun in bed. They're not above roughhousing, wrestling, tickling and giggling, sometimes simultaneously. In fact, they find the act of laughing to be *tres* arousing. I've heard reports that Sag guys and gals can actually get stiff or sodden after some good guffawing.

Sex games are fine for Sags, just so long as they're not too involved or time-consuming. The Archer's love of flitting from one thing to the next continues in the boudoir. But Sagittarius absolutely hates being tied up or restrained in any way. It seriously freaks them out and can send them packing. Perhaps this is rooted in their horse-self, a revolt against being domesticated. So just remember, no ties! Literally.

You won't need to play a guessing game to find out what turns the Archer on—they'll tell you, straight up. Some have gotten the rep of being selfish lovers, which is unfortunate, because in the sack, Sags can be very giving. Although they're extremely direct and forthcoming about their own needs, Sagittarians have no problem satisfying yours. Just don't beat around the bush because they have no patience for coyness in bed. Let them know just what you want and you'll get it—and get it thoroughly.

If you seek a serious lover with plenty of romance, keep looking. Sagittarius like to cut to the chase and get down and dirty with little ceremony. While they're not big on foreplay, they make up for it with endurance.

Many Sags can also be talented in the area of oral pleasure. They take the acts of fellatio or cunnilingus luxuriously slow and steady, which I equate with their horse-half's penchant for grazing. Imagine the methodical way a pony munches in a field and you'll get a picture of Sag's style.

The term "hung like a horse" brings to mind the Sagittarius man because they are usually especially well endowed. Even short in stature Sags have been known to sport impressive packages. Plus I've been told that they can go at it like prize breeding stallions. Not surprisingly, doggie-style is their fave position—which, in their case, can also be called "horsy-style." But most Centaurs aren't adverse to a little Cowgirl and being taken out on the range for a long, hard ride.

Relationship wise, tread lightly with Sagittarians. Though they are not opposed to settling down, all too often, they equate commitment with confinement. They are easy to bed but tough to wed because of their fear that marriage might put the kibosh on the freedom they hold so near and dear to their big hearts.

Make no mistake, though—Sags aren't against monogamy or opposed to being fully devoted to one partner but they're terrified of feeling trapped. Once they meet a partner who understands their need for freedom, they are happy to roam but even happier to come home to your welcoming bed.

Sagittarian spontaneity between the sheets is legendary. Hooking up with a Sag in the sack is almost always an tremendously satisfying union for both parties, the perfect combination of fire and fun—and fiery fun. Think multiple orgasms with an daring partner that just won't quit and an adventurous soul to boot.

The Sagittarius Diet

A tough Sun Sign to pin down culinarily, Sagittarius' eating habits are yet another example of its horse-half wrestling with its human-half. While some Sags enjoy a meat-free, grain-heavy meal plan, others are carnivores supreme. Ray contends that the best diet for the Centaur is a balanced one, a happy medium between fleshy proteins, healthy whole grains and farm-fresh veggies.

Suffice to say that Sagittarians enjoy fragrant, exotic, yet ballsy foods. Moroccan stews which include a touch of meat, legumes like chick peas or lentils with perhaps a fruity twist like apples or apricots, are real belly-pleasers for them. Ditto for *bouillabaisse* and its Italian cousin *cioppino*, with its savory blend of seafood, tomatoes and tender veggies. An interesting palate with variety in every bite which smacks of world travel and tastes of adventure is what draws the Archer to the table.

Since they tend to be extremely physically active, Sagittarians don't traditionally have trouble with their weight—the rare sedentary Sags do. With their quick metabolisms, they burn off what they eat, and what they eat is usually pretty healthy.

Lean and slender in their youth, the Archer's frame sometimes tends to thicken as they age. Females in particular can put on weight in their ruling Bodyparts—hips and thighs—but they wear it well. However, if they do nothing but move around a bit more, they usually see a dramatic change and trim down with little effort.

For lustrous hair, skin and gums (areas that suffer most when a Sagittarian eats poorly), eating the skins of fruits and vegetables are important for them. So don't peel those apples and potatoes! Raw salads, green peppers, figs and strawberries are especially key. A high-protein diet is also beneficial for the Archer, so in addition to red meat, remember broiled poultry, fish and eggs.

Because of their fast metabolisms, Sagittarians are often hungry throughout the day, so "grazing" on handfuls of nuts or grapes and mini-meals seem to suit their on-the-go lifestyles and keep them feeling full but not stuffed to the brim.

Sags don't digest dairy well. Likewise for heavy, fatty foods like cream-based sauces on pasta or gravies. A large percentage of Archers are lactose intolerant and don't even know it. Ray's rule of the kitchen, "If it don't feel good, don't eat it!" rings particularly true for the relationship between dairy and Sagittarius.

Alcohol also doesn't sit well with Centaurs and besides doing damage to their livers faster than most other signs of the Zodiac, it does a job on their highly sensitive skin by making it blotchy and mottled. So Sags must take care to limit alcohol, or better yet, avoid it completely.

A good rule of thumb for Sagittarians is to stick with foods and liquids that a horse might eat or drink...those in their purest form—clear water, garden-fresh fruits and veggies and additive-free grains. When indulging in meat products and poultry, then grass-fed is best.

Capricorn
December 22 – January 20

Element: Earth

Heavenly Body: Saturn

Symbol: The Goat

Stone: Garnet

Lifequest: To do themselves proud

Vibe: Strong and stubborn

Dirty Little Secret: I don't want you to like me, just respect me.

Bodypart: Bones (including joints, knees and teeth)

Fuelfoods: Nothing fancy, just straight-up staples like roasted chicken and burgers suit them fine.

Sign Song: "You're the Top"

Movie: *Forrest Gump*—The saga of a simple man who overcomes adversities with kindness, fortitude, common sense and love is reminiscent of a Capricorn heart.

All About Capricorn

Many regard Capricorn as the tip top of the Zodiac. Why? Their symbolic representation is the goat, a creature that's associated with slowly, methodically, quietly and sure-footedly making it to the apex of the mountaintop. In the same way, Capricorn the Goat's relentless pursuit of anything and everything they desire and their general determination, is legendary.

However, there are two radically-different types of Capricorns among Sun Signs:

- **The Mountain Goat** – This courageous soul is always striving to new heights until they reach the pinnacle and they aren't satisfied until they're viewing the world from on high; and

- **The Barnyard Goat** – Content to be king (or queen) over a very small, comfortable domain, this domesticated critter is the poster child of an underachiever. "Just enough" is more than enough for them.

But no matter which type, all Capricorns are amazingly patient and they continue to persist no matter what the odds. They bring to mind Winston Churchill's mantras, "Never, never, never give up" and "If you're walking through hell, keep going." Though Sir Winnie was a Sagittarius, I believe he embodied the soul of a Capricorn with quotes like this.

Caps know that even the arduous, most treacherous trip starts with one step and they are more than willing to take that step — even if they know the journey will be mostly uphill and rocky. These persistent Goats almost always reach their goal because they keep their eye on the pinnacle and the sky beyond.

Far from being Sagittarius dreamers, Capricorns are excellent at achieving their dreams and rarely, if ever, getting disheartened. However, Caps don't have the knack for balancing work and play like Libras do, so unless they're incredibly focused, they can get distracted and go off on a side trail. If this is the case, it might take them a little longer to reach the top and they might get cut and bruised along the way, but they do make it. Eventually.

Being an Earth Sign, Capricorns can struggle with their footing. Unless you're extremely adept, maneuvering a rocky road is a difficult feat to master. Stony surfaces can get slick, the dirt path can get washed out and be difficult to follow, so it's easy to lose your way. But the Goat's determination, surefootedness and inexorable spirit usually carries them through.

Capricorns are also "the top" of whatever career they choose. As the most likely Sun Sign to be workaholics, they often neglect their personal lives in favor of the job. It's not unusual for a Capricorn to miss their child's dance recital because of a late meeting or for them to turn a romantic getaway into a working vacation. The possibility of missing a deadline or the risk of failing at a new task is simply not in their vocabulary.

Hopelessly traditional and wary, Capricorns aren't adverse to trying creative, new avenues to achieve their goals. Be it for booty or business, the Goat is unrelenting until they get what they want. As you can imagine, this sure-footed, plodding creature is most comfortable with a steady beau and tends to stay in a job forever, sometimes long after the blush is off the rose.

Famed Capricorns include Susan Lucci, Kit Carson, Ryan Seacrest, Clara Barton, Anwar Sadat, Annie Lennox, Mao Zedong, Henry Miller, Aaliyah, Louis Pasteur, Marlene Dietrich, Denzel Washington, Sandy Koufax, Patti Smith, Rudyard

Kipling, Henri Matisse, Gypsy Rose Lee, Isaac Asimov, Joan of Arc, Buzz Aldrin, Mel Gibson, Kate Moss, Isaac Newton, Janis Joplin, David Bowie, Elvis Presley, Martin Luther King, Dolly Parton, Paul Cezanne, Mary J. Blige, Al Capone, Dido, Federico Fellini, Benjamin Franklin and Muhammad Ali. All at the top of their game, right?

For Capricorn, Saturn rules. Now, this is a planet that represents conscientiousness, organization and determination. Even Goats that work, work, work are blessed with a bountiful spirit. Caps are also known for their wicked sense of humor which has a tendency to be offbeat and a bit off color but is always good-natured and never mean-spirited. Although Capricorns might look "all business" on the outside, deep down they're really party animals. They know how to cut loose!

Capricorns are the entrepreneurs among us. They are the bosses, the managers, the captains and sergeants. However, even when they are in positions of lower authority, Caps display "take charge" leadership characteristics.

As you might imagine, the driving force behind the Goat is winning—position, wealth and power—and not necessarily in that order. They're natural born leaders. When tasked with leading a team (even an inexperienced one) up a treacherous mountain path, under Capricorn's watchful eye and guidance, everyone makes it up to the peak in one piece and in record time.

Pragmatic, motivated and highly-structured, Capricorn is the one who can get your disastrous office humming like a busy bee and organize your mess of a walk-in closet into a true thing of wonder. They are also master jugglers, fearlessly taking on a number of projects at once and seeing each one to a magnificent conclusion.

Driven and goal-oriented, as a pal or a partner, Capricorns can be counted on through thick and thin, to help you laugh through tears and weather even the darkest storm. They not only like hard work, but they thrive upon it. Without a conflict or a struggle to wrestle with, the Goat is often lost, so it's best to keep them busy, occupied and always climbing toward the stars.

Capricorn Between the Sheets

No-nonsense Capricorn prefers their sex the same way as they like everything else—straight up, no chaser, no frills. This is why missionary position is their favorite, because it's simple, no nonsense and gets the job done.

Other erotic postures Caps can get down with are seated (feet flat on the ground) and rear-entry. Most of the animal-based signs (especially Aries and to a lesser extent Sagittarius) have an affinity for doing the nasty like a dog, or in this case, like a barnyard goat.

It's not to say that Caps are only interested in "vanilla sex," because they can get freaky with the best of them. These lovers of power are especially adept at role-playing scenarios that involve authority. Pass the handcuffs, please! Punishing police officer and speeding motorist is a fave, closely followed by naughty student and strict teacher. To shake things up once in a while, Caps might even be game to play the "bottom" and let somebody else take charge, but only occasionally.

The Goat tends to gravitate toward older, more experienced partners, people who are on par with them sexually and possess authority and expertise. Although they aren't averse to playing the teacher either. As an erotic educator, Capricorns can be patient, thorough and especially skilled in this role.

There's no doubt about it, Capricorns are strong, powerful lovers. Think sinewy barnyard animals. Again, like the other animal signs, the men can go at it for hours and possess impressive stamina. Firmly grounded, Capricorn females love to take the superior position and squat onto their partner (face or genitals) which gives them a feeling of supremacy. And power, as you know, gets them off.

Capricorns need a mate that makes them feel secure. Only then can the sharp goat's horns break away to reveal the tender, faithful heart that beats beneath. Cap's cautious nature causes them to tread lightly when embarking upon a new love. They are tentative, testing the ground before putting their full weight into the relationship. After which, they're yours forever.

Did you know that the word "horny," meaning easily aroused, is a reference to the horns of a goat? That explains a lot about this Sun Sign. Unfortunately, many Goats have a tough time with monogamy. Their mode of thought is that more is more—the more lovers, the more cars, the more orgasms—and that more is better. But it's also possible for, Capricorns to be faithful, devoted lovers...with the right partner.

So key is Capricorn's quest for success and to be "the top," that they sometimes won't bust a move until they're 100% sure of success. In other words, if a Goat sees a person they're attracted to, they won't take a chance and ask them out unless they're absolutely certain they won't be turned down. Sadly, this tunnel vision might result in lost opportunities for them. But taking chances is a big no-no in their book.

Good matches for Capricorns are Scorpio, Taurus and Virgo, because each brings something to the table that the Goat requires. The latter two are similarly grounded Earth Signs but Scorpio's Water sensibilities help dilute Cap's sometimes strong behavior. As a rule, Capricorns do better with other Earth Signs but I've witnessed many happy unions between the Water Signs of Cancer, Pisces and Scorpio—especially Scorpio, as noted above.

Although they do their best to appear staid and reserved on the outside, have no doubt that these satyr-like creatures can get kinky...if they let themselves. Caps who follow these desires might even entertain fetishes that others consider taboo. Where they fall on the star charts indicate their degree of interest in BDSM (bondage and discipline, sadism and masochism) but nine times out of 10 Caps are interested, even fleetingly, in the dark avenues of love.

Because Saturn, their ruling planet, is a hard taskmaster, some Caps might be under a great deal of internal pressure. Sexual abandon is one way they can help diffuse their intense energies, Dr. Vivian suggests. But Capricorns are happiest embracing their inner Goat and letting their freak flag fly.

Because their ruling Bodypart is their beautiful bones, Capricorn's legs are extremely sensitive, especially the knees. If you lightly stimulate the ticklish backs of their knees, they will shiver with delight. It's an excellent type of foreplay that Caps are extremely responsive to. They might even get super-aroused by licking their way up and down a partner's legs, along their inner thighs, just stopping at the genitals, a maddening but delicious game.

While they're not exactly high maintenance, the Goat does need lots of praise and reassurance in the bedroom. Their quest to be the best, extends to their erotic endeavors. The good news is that Capricorns won't give up until their partner is completely satisfied.

The Capricorn Diet

Most Capricorns prefer foods that are traditional, nothing fancy. Roasted chicken suits them fine. In fact, chicken prepared any which way is often one of their favorite dishes. They might even boast a status-conscious palate for rich cuts of beef like filet mignon and crown roasts. You know, the Capricorn quest for the top even extends to the best of foods.

Given a choice, these Goats will opt for meat over all else, which isn't the healthiest for their constitutions. To balance their love of the flesh, vitamin C consumption is in order. Oranges, lemons, figs, dandelion greens, spinach and broccoli are good selections. A diet high in protein and calcium is a must to keep their bones strong because even though bones are the Goat's ruling Bodypart, Capricorns are prone to bone breaks and brittleness. Cheese, buttermilk and yogurt should be a regular part of their daily diet.

Creatures of habit, Capricorns can fall into an eating rut, reaching for the same foods every day or the same succession of foods each week. I'm referring to pattern eating like Monday is Spaghetti Day, Tuesday is Meatloaf Day and so on. Variety keeps them on an even keel, even if it might take a bit of coercing to put a bit of spice into their diets.

While Caps do like spicy foods, fiery foods don't like them back and they're prone to intestinal distress when the piquant line is crossed. Indulging in heavy foods is also a no-no. Think goat diet. No, not the fact that these bovines are known to chomp on tin cans plus whatever else crosses their path. But the fact is that they will eat almost any kind of plant material.

Unfortunately, I have some bad news—Earth Signs have a tendency to be overweight. But with Capricorn, glandular problems are more typically the culprit than overeating. Their weight struggle can be aggravated by too little exercise and a sedentary lifestyle. They must be urged out of the armchair and out of the barnyard and into an existence which includes a bit of exercising.

Hiking is an especially good physical activity for Capricorns, who really take to it once they start. Trekking long distances up rugged terrain is a natural for them. It also helps ground them, most importantly, when they find themselves pushing too hard. That's the time they should stretch their legs, head to the hills and embrace their inner Goat.

Aquarius
January 21 – February 19

Element: Air

Heavenly Body: Uranus

Symbol: The Water Bearer

Stone: Amethyst

Lifequest: To be all seeing, all knowing

Vibe: Full throttle

Dirty Little Secret: I want to be unique; normal scares me.

Bodyparts: Circulatory system and ankles
(including the calves and shins)

Fuelfoods: Anything seafood (surprise!), especially sushi, and
liquidy meals like chowders

Sign Song: "Aquarius/Let the Sunshine In"

Movie: *August Rush*—This whimsical tale of a music prodigy
whose inner magic touches all around him captures the Aquarius
spark.

All About Aquarius

Those born under the Sun Sign of Aquarius actually radiate with an inner light. Literally. If their hair isn't blonde, then their skin has a warm glow (even it's deep brown) or their eyes shine with beneficence and intelligence. Aquarians are ready to take on the world—and do, with style, panache, heart and kindness.

With the birth of the new Millennium in 2000, the "Age of Aquarius" was heralded. And more than 30 years earlier, it was saluted with the joyous song from the Broadway musical *Hair*, which captures the sign's promise and exuberance.

Each astrological "age" results from the achingly slow revolution of the Earth's rotation and is approximately 2,150 years in length. But unlike the Signs of the Zodiac, these ages move in the opposite direction, so the previous Age of Pisces was followed by Aquarius.

Because of this, the humble Water Bearer of the star charts is regarded as the Zodiac's leader. This means Aquarians are the guiding light for the future. An awesome responsibility but Aquarius takes it all in stride, with confidence, never spilling a drop of the precious lifeblood it is entrusted to carry.

Aquarians are also *mucho moderne* thanks to their ruling planet, Uranus, which is often associated with electricity and other revolutionary inventions. The planet was discovered around the time of the Industrial Revolution, which is one reason for this. Uranus' electric connection explains why Aquarius has got to be the first kid on the block with a new iPhone, computer or App. It's simply in their nature.

Many believe that those born under Aquarius dance to their own inner music—and it's never the same dance or song. They're constantly reinventing themselves, improving themselves, and in the process, making a deeper mark upon those around them. The Aquarius mind is always hurtling forward, even when they should be at rest, which explains why a large number are insomniacs. They can have a difficult time finding—and using—their "off" button!

Because of their preoccupation with the mind and things intellectual, Aquarians find themselves in the good company of inventors and innovators, and people who make their mark. Oprah Winfrey, Charles Darwin, Paul Newman, Franklin D. Roosevelt, Anton Chekov, Abraham Lincoln, Babe Ruth, Gregory Hines, Charles Dickens, Bob Marley, Jennifer Aniston, Etta and Rick James, Philip Glass, Mikhail Baryshnikov, John Carradine, Hank Aaron, Amy Tan, James Dean, Sheryl Crow, Thomas Edison, Jules Verne, Mozart and Michael Jordan are all Water Bearers.

A couple of compelling Aquarian facts: In the American Hall of Fame, you'll find a larger number of Aquarians than any other Sun Sign but mental institutions also have a greater number of Water Bearers as well. This is a sign of extremes, which can take Aquarius to some amazing and some very bleak places. For them, the glass is either full or empty.

Aquarius is also a philanthropic sign. Among their ranks are supreme caregivers like doctors, nurses, counselors and home attendants. When wealthy, Water Bearers support several causes. Even when they're not mega-rich like Oprah, Aquarians tend to have deep pockets for needy causes and often volunteer their valuable time. They are known to flourish in "make a difference" careers where their daily labors truly make a positive impact upon people's lives—but to Water Bearers, it's hardly work at all.

In addition to being extremely charitable, Aquarians also offer refreshingly objective points of view. Although highly emotional, they never let their personal feelings obstruct their decisions. They also have a knack for helping others to see the validity of their arguments, so they're great mediators, even in the most heated discussions.

Gregarious and likable, everyone wants to be the Water Bearer's friend. And of friends they have many. It's not unusual for them to have thousands of Facebook Friends, and to keep up with all of them. People seem to flock to Aquarius and in turn, Water Bearers make particularly faithful, giving buddies.

But because of the unpredictable nature of Uranus, they sometimes have explosive tempers which flare up with little advance warning. (In mythology, Uranus was such an SOB that his wife Gaia, aka Mother Earth, fashioned a special sickle so that his own son could castrate him! And you think your family's messed up.) This Air Sign can rise up like a sudden tornado, then dissipate just as quickly, leaving a wake of destruction in its path.

Ruled by the almost featureless planet Uranus, those born under Aquarius are often astrology's most baffling and bizarre— but not in a bad way. These Water Bearers vary immensely and like seashells on a beach, they'll each be very, very different.

Although others might dub the Aquarian mode of thought and deeds as unusual, it's this nonconformity that makes them such awesome individuals. They strive to stand out, to be unique. Nothing scares an Aquarius more than being considered "normal." That's when they'll do something edgy, wacky and unexplainable just to be considered "out there."

However, it can to be difficult to follow the Aquarian mode of thought sometimes because their minds work so quickly, flitting from one idea to the next in a matter of seconds. At first, they might seem to be off topic, but then they'll pull it all together with an innovative mode of thought you never considered. Aquarians will commonly have you nodding your head in wonder and admitting, "I never thought of that."

Aquarians are also great activists. They're the ones at protests, carrying inventive signs. They're the ones who will support a political candidate (usually, the winning candidate) as a volunteer. They're the ones saving the whales and the planet. Water Bearers are happiest when they're active and have something to support.

Definitely not a passive member of the Zodiac, most will be thrilled to move through life with this wonderfully exciting Sun Sign. Perfect mates for Aquarius include Gemini and Libra. The duality of these signs seem to adapt well to the Aquarian's changeability and volatility.

Aquarius Between the Sheets

The mirror opposite of their sweet and sunny demeanor, in the bedroom, Aquarians take on a totally different persona. They can be downright kinky in many people's eyes—although as Dr. Vivian points out, we don't judge here, just try to inform.

Aquarius folks try to put forth a nonchalant attitude about sex because they want to project the image that they can take it or leave it, but in reality, Aquarians are extremely lusty. Horn dogs and sex kittens, if you will—that is, if those statements aren't too judgmental.

But for Water Bearers, it's never rutting without substance. Things erotic are intensely deep and personal for them. Just like they can be prone to overthink and intellectualize everything else in their lives, Aquarius puts a great deal of brainpower into the sex act.

Without beating around the bush, I'll just come out and say it—many Aquarians are into anal sex. Its social stigma attracts them as do the sensations which are hyper-intense, bordering on pain and complex. Even straight Aquarian men crave a digit or two inserted deep past the knuckle every now and again. Many Aquarius ladies report that they can achieve orgasm solely from anal stimulation, much to the delight of their partners. Aquarians are turned on by the taboo.

While some Water Bearers are disturbed by this fact, most are not. Vivian encourages everyone, no matter their Sun Sign, to embrace their personal erotic proclivities, even those that religious sects and most societies consider deviant. ("I mean, oral sex is still technically illegal in many US states and most people consider it 'normal,'" she laughs.)

Although they might appear cool and nonplussed in bed, Aquarians are generally adept lovers and are extremely open-minded. They hold their passion deep inside and they try their best to contain their excitement, which they fear makes them appear vulnerable. Being horny, in their eyes, is losing control.

This is one reason that "sex from afar" is so appealing to Water Bearers. They are drawn to phone and cyber sex because they both create a safe distance—from themselves and from their messy passion. Since Aquarians are very heady (the big thinkers of the Zodiac), the idea of detachment is a huge turn-on for them.

So, disembodied erotic encounters, a faceless voice on the telephone or engorged, unattached genitals on a video monitor offer Aquarius a perfect escape. Men, in particular, may carry on lengthy private chat room trysts that get hot and heavy, yet don't jeopardize their marriages or serious relationships.

When Aquarians indulge in role-playing romps, a favorite theme is cuckold fantasies. (Remember the whole cuckold thing from Chaucer, et al? "Being cuckolded" is Middle English for being played. But these days, cuckolding means not just having an unfaithful spouse, Dr. Vivian points out, but actually getting aroused by watching your partner partake in another.) So cuckold away, Aquarians!

This could mean setting up an encounter with another man or woman that the spouse watches from a clandestine spot, unbeknownst to the other partner. Or it could mean that the "other" is in on the whole thing. Often, this type of threeway relationship can endure for many happy years.

Even though the Water Bearer is not a Water Sign, they have certain water elements, especially in the sack. Aquarius gals are often gushers—that's right, they actually spurt copious amounts of a thick, clear liquid when they climax. While this might put off some timid partners, others take it as the rare gift it is.

I remember a cousin confiding in me that he once dated a lady who was a gusher. When I asked what happened to her, Billy gave me a wicked grin and said, "I married her!" And wouldn't you know it, Ang was an Aquarius through and through.

Likewise, a good number of Aquarius men are right up there with their female counterparts, blessed with intense and bountiful emissions.

Because those born under this auspicious sign also tend to be very wise and knowing, they see the spark in potential partners that others do not. They are particularly attracted to those branded offbeat or odd. Physical differences don't faze them—they have the gift of looking beyond the fact that someone may have a prominent scar, lost a limb or has dwarfism, and are able to see the unique, special qualities in someone society labels "disabled."

The Aquarius Diet

Extremely social beings, Aquarians are a welcome addition to any dinner party. They make everyone feel so relaxed and at home because they're so comfortable within their own skins. Though not adventurous eaters like Aries, Aquarians are curious about new things and will give unusual cuisines like Ethiopian a whirl when none of your other friends will.

Aquarius encompasses aspects of many other Sun Signs and incorporate facets of the three other Elements. I like to say that Water Bearers possess the best qualities from the rest of the Zodiac. Though oddly enough, not a Water Sign, Aquarius has an appreciation for seafood. Sushi is a favorite, especially its seaweed and kelp components.

Water Bearers absolutely love one-pot, soupy meals like hearty chowders. Clam (red or white) chowders, creamy corn soups, lobster bisques, even simple potato purees are what they crave. They prefer these over thicker, more substantial food selections like chilis or stews.

Aquarius also likes to mix cuisines, which some Sun Signs, like veggie Virgo or typical Taurus, find repugnant. But Aquarians think nothing of having guacamole for the first course, then ravioli and a gooey slice of German chocolate cake for dessert.

Healthwise, Aquarians are generally hale and strong. They have good muscle and hand-eye coordination and well-formed legs. Because one of their ruling Bodyparts is the ankles, they're usually excellent at sports like soccer and lacrosse. But they're also prone to circulatory problems, so a healthy Water Bearer is an active one.

Because they're usually so busy, Aquarians are big snackers. For them, it's easier to grab and go than to sit down for a meal. So instead of reaching for chips or a candy bar, it's a much healthier option for them to chow down on a handful of nuts or blueberries. And for all of us!

A balanced diet for the Water Bearer should include ocean delights like tuna, lobster and oysters plus vegetables like spinach, radishes, celery, cabbage, a variety of lettuce and squash. Nuts like almonds and walnuts are also recommended as are fruits like apples, peaches, pears, lemons and oranges, with the occasional exotic fruit like pineapple, pomegranate and kiwi, thrown in for good measure. Although dairy products are also important, many Aquarians don't process milk products well, but cultured calcium products like yogurt are especially well tolerated.

Pisces
February 20 – March 20

Element: Water

Heavenly Body: Neptune

Symbol: The Fish

Stone: Bloodstone

Lifequest: To be loved, accepted unconditionally and feel part of a group

Vibe: Inconsistent energy, full of peaks and valleys

Dirty Little Secret: I am on a constant quest to make my dreams a reality.

Bodypart: The feet

Fuelfoods: Another seafood lover but with a touch of spice like gumbo or Lobster Fra Diavolo

Sign Song: "Nature Boy"

Movie: *The Old Man and the Sea*—A parable of man versus nature, (like Don Quixote on the ocean), the old man here has Piscean determination and never gives up, even when all seems lost.

All About Pisces

Just like ocean creatures travel in schools, so too does Pisces, the Zodiac's finned resident, feel most comfortable being part of a group. In fact, this search for a sense of belonging is a large factor in the Fish's lifequest—to be cherished, accepted no matter what, and to feel like they belong. A tall order but Pisces won't feel secure or "right" unless they fit in.

Think of how elusive fish are: moving quickly, sometimes visible just below the water's surface, then gone in a flash. Pisces are among the most puzzling and yet the most appealing of the dozen Sun Signs.

Just when you think you've got a Pisces "hooked" (in a relationship or friendship), they dart off and you don't see them again until they're good and ready to be seen. For the Fish, it's an eternal inner battle—wanting to be loved but making it very difficult to love them because they skitter off when anyone gets close.

Those born under the auspices of Pisces gravitate toward the arts, particularly writing, music and acting, because careers in these areas allow them to be elusive and change their personas from role to role and piece to piece.

Although Pisceans tend to be extremely talented in their chosen careers, they spend most of their lives fighting conflicts. It can get so bad that they threaten to stonewall themselves and are their own worst enemies. Why do the Fish consistently miss deadlines? Why are they often late to rehearsals? I'll bet even Pisces can't even answer why the sign tends to be so self-destructive. But I can help shed some light on this mystery.

Picture Pisces' Sign Symbol…it's not merely one fish but two fish—and two fish that are headed in opposite directions. This illustrates the Piscean's never-ending struggle within itself and its tendencies to self-implode.

Yes, the Fish are their own worst enemies. They are saint and sinner rolled into one. Remember the scene in the film noir classic *The Night of the Hunter* when sexy sociopath Robert Mitchum's hands, tattooed with the words "love" and "hate," battle each other? That's a perfect illustration of the 12th sign of the Zodiac, immersed in a continual war with itself.

In their careers, Pisceans can be visionaries or disenchanted drones, the genius in a penthouse apartment or in the homeless shelter, the professor or the psychotic. Notable Pisceans include George Washington, Renoir, Rupert Murdoch, Czar Alexander III, Henrik Ibsen, Frederic Chopin, Barbie, Spike Lee, Kurt Cobain, Anais Nin, Michelangelo, Rihanna, Jack Kerouac, Eva Longoria, George Harrison, Ansel Adams, Bruce Willis, Liza Minnelli, Johnny Cash, Cindy Crawford, Sidney Poitier, Ke$ha, Albert Einstein, John Steinbeck, Shannon Tweed, Queen Latifah, Chaz Bono and Alexander Graham Bell. See what I mean?

But I bow in acknowledgement to Pisces. Despite their slew of challenging characteristics, they are incredibly talented, resilient and adaptable. It's not unusual to find that the Fish are leaders in the varied fields they have chosen to pursue. The Fortune 500 list is brimming with them—but so are correctional institutions.

It's sad but true but unfortunately, prisons, reform schools and the like statistically are home to a large number of Pisceans. Many astrologers attribute this fact to what is known as the

"Ivory Tower Syndrome." For Pisces, this represents an unattainable quest, setting sights too high and thus, being destined for failure. Things always look better from that fabled Ivory Tower—if I just accomplish this or that then I'll finally be happy. And the Fish's determination often does win them what they seek. However, when they get it, they're still unfulfilled. Why? Because they fail to find the joy within themselves.

A big part of a Piscean's life takes place in their own private fantasyland. They constantly daydream about situations and people—especially folks they're attracted to romantically—and can find themselves in the lurch because they spend so much time thinking and not enough time doing. A very talented Piscean writer friend of ours logs more hours talking about the book he's working on than actually writing it. Ten years later, he still hasn't written more than 50 pages.

Since Pisces can exist so completely in their own personal La-La Land, they can be in the dark about what's going on right under their noses. So much so that their mates can easily carry on affairs without them having a clue. Pisces is a Sun Sign of great wonders and sometimes, even greater disappointment. But please don't take this as a criticism but merely a warning.

For Pisces, their emotions can be their Achilles heel (after all, they are ruled by their feet) but they also have amazing qualities. They're imaginative and sensitive, compassionate and kind, selfless and innocent, intuitive and empathetic. Pisces will go out of their way to help a friend and take on the burden of their problems as though they're their own.

Of all the signs of the Zodiac, Pisces is the most psychic. Many of their problems arise when they ignore their instincts and go against their hunches.

They're also one of the most likely Sun Signs to have drug and alcohol addictions and other indulgences. For Pisces, substance abuse is a way to let down their guard, escape life's pressures and get more in tune with their spiritual side. Piscean addiction is less about weakness and more about choice. When they decide to change their wayward ways, they demonstrate fortitude and success like no other Sun Sign. In addition to being abusers, they are also some of the most successful Twelve-Steppers you'll ever want to meet.

Influenced by Neptune (the planet and the Roman sea god), Pisces can be deep and mysterious, yet has a sensitivity beyond measure. Perhaps the trouble is that Pisces feels too deeply and too much.

Because Neptune transformed himself into a stallion to seduce the goddess Demeter, he is also considered by some to be the inventor of horse-racing—so gambling addictions, especially playing the ponies, aren't uncommon in this Zodiac sign. Pisces has an extremely addictive personality so they need to be careful in this area as well.

As astrology's most sensitive sign, Pisces takes everything to heart, so they benefit greatly from disappearing on mini vacations in order to deal with life's pressures. Then they come back refreshed, refueled and raring to go.

Pisces is also the most liquid of the Water Signs, suggesting constant change and flux, especially of spirit. They make incredible friends and caring mates, however they often look after others more thoughtfully than they look after themselves. It takes a special partner to help the Fish overcome their inner obstacles. Scorpio, Cancer and Virgo (and sometimes

Capricorn) are usually up to the challenge and find Pisces to be an extremely rewarding partner and a lifelong friend.

Pisces Between the Sheets

In some circles, the twin fish is known as "the Sign of the Flirt" because they are perhaps the biggest charmers of the Zodiac. But mostly, it's just an ego-booster for Pisces, a game, and most Fish do love games.

Erotically, Pisceans are game for almost anything and especially love getting dirty. This Water Sign knows that a little soap, water and elbow grease can remove even the nastiest stains. I wouldn't go so far as to say that nothing turns them off but...

A large number of Fish have urolagnia fetishes, tells Dr. Vivian—that is, they are aroused by urination. Now, this is an extensive fetish with many facets, including getting sexual pleasure from watching another person urinate or being urinated upon (aka "golden showers"), so it's much too complicated to go into great detail here. But the Piscean fascination with pee is so common that it warrants a mention.

For more about fetishes like urolagnia, we highly recommend the books, *Fetish and You* and *Sex, Fetish and Him*.

Another fetishy area for Pisces is the feet, their ruling Bodypart. Plain and simple, the Fish dig feet—meaning that they get hot looking at, touching, smelling and massaging the feet (and/or go over the moon for a foot massage themselves). Some even enjoy inserting a big toe "where the sun doesn't shine." Piscean guys report loving to slide themselves between a pair of well-oiled female feet. And I haven't met a Pisces lady yet who doesn't have a zillion pairs of shoes in their closet. The same is true for some Pisces gents too.

Dr. V says that the message here is anything goes. As long as both adults are of age and are willing, the rule of thumb is, if it feels good, do it!

For Pisces, the physical and the emotional are intertwined so they can be very serious about sex. Perhaps too serious. When things are going well romantically, Pisces is on top of the world but when relationships take a downturn, they literally fall apart. If their love life takes a nosedive, it affects everything else in their life and can even prompt them to question their very existence. It can go as far as to drive them to thoughts of suicide. We urge you to seek professional help if this scenario hits close to home. Wanting to kill yourself is never normal behavior. Do know that help is there if you need it—and please take advantage of it. And we can help you find it.

No matter their personal proclivities, Pisces are chameleons in the bedroom. They can be ultra romantic and mushy one moment, then withdrawn and distant the next. But take note that Pisces are pleasers and this means that they're usually very skilled and passionate lovers.

The Pisces Diet

At the dining room table, Pisces loves all things seafood. No surprise here, right? Since they are one of the Zodiac's most creative signs, they are all about a food's presentation. In other words, they care about the way an entree is arranged on a plate and might actually turn down a dish that is quite wonderful because it doesn't look "right." To them, food presentation illustrates all of the care that went into creating it and its potential deliciousness factor.

Besides presentation, another key word for Pisces is savory. They're not big fans of the fiery and the zingy but do like flavorful foods created with an interesting array of spices. Traditionally, Pisces love dishes like paella just so long as it's not bitingly hot. Pisceans aren't adverse to ingredients like cumin or curry, just not large amounts. And they absolutely love the fresh, green flavor of cilantro and mint.

Pisces' senses of taste and smell are extremely acute, so if something is the tiniest bit "off," the Fish won't eat it even if they're absolutely starving. Pisces are the ones who madden cooks by sniffing the stuff on their plate or fork, so if they don't find the fragrance appetizing, they will politely refuse to eat it. Or send things back to a restaurant kitchen instead of suffering through a sub-par meal.

As children, Pisceans might have been labeled fussy eaters but this isn't exactly accurate. I'd venture to say that they have sophisticated palates, even as grown-ups. Distinguished tastes... now doesn't that sound better?

Pisces are open-minded eaters in the sense that they're willing to try different cuisines and that they like a variety of unconventional flavors. Many enjoy dishes flavored with rosewater and orange blossom water. They usually love the earthiest, mustiest-tasting truffles and the strongest-tasting sushi like saba (mackerel).

Since Pisces are prone to low iron, the iron-rich choices they crave—like seafood—are a good bet for them. Also recommended are liver, kidneys, lean beef, lamb and oysters. Low cholesterol whole grain cereals, barley and all types of beans are also excellent. They shouldn't forget greens like dark lettuces and spinach, and also dried fruits like raisins and dates, plus fresh fruits like apricots, peaches, grapes, apples, lemons and oranges.

Salt—even sea salt—should be limited because it causes Pisceans to retain water. They are also particularly sensitive to caffeine, especially coffee, so it should be kept to a bare minimum.

The Fish are also very susceptible to the effects of alcohol—they're what my dad would call a "cheap drunk." Even one drink can do them in. So, for Pisces, the term "to drink like a fish" is not the least bit accurate.

As with all the Sun Signs mentioned in this book, the best diet is a balanced diet with helpings from the five food groups, and a healthy indulgence from their Fuelfoods.

Closing Thoughts

We hope with all of our hearts that you've found what you were looking for in the *Astrology Sex Diet* and that it helps guide you safely and happily along your intended path in your life's journey and beyond. It was written with much love, careful consideration and good intentions. May you find inner peace and a deeper understanding of yourself and those around you.

We look forward to your feedback.

- Ariella, Vivian & Ray

Like us on Facebook
and follow our monthly posts to further guide you.

Other Books From Volossal Publishing

Humor
Is Your Boyfriend Really Your Girlfriend?
You Might Be A Douchebag
You Might Be A Metalhead
You're Probably A Slut
Online Dating Advice from The Match Master
Cartoons That Will Send Me Straight To Hell

Novels
The El
Different Drummer
The Lunch

Biographies
And Then I S**t My Pants
Jesus, Hitler, Manson and Me
A Boy In Hiding

Self Help/Relationship Advice
Fetish and You
Sex, Fetish and Him
Why Not If It Works
You've Got The Balls, Use Them!
Confessions of a Fat Player

Cooking
Tamales For Gringos
Feeding The Beast

Volossal Publishing
www.volossal.com

www.ingramcontent.com/pod-product-compliance
Lightning Source LLC
Chambersburg PA
CBHW070806100426
42742CB00012B/2269